Moving

A play

Hugh Leonard

Samuel French – London
New York – Hollywood – Toronto

ISBN 0 573 01837 5

Please see page iv for further copyright information.

MOVING

First presented at the Abbey Theatre, Dublin, on 21st April 1992, with the following cast of characters:

Removals Man	Johnny Murphy
His Assistant	Gerry McCann
Ellie Noone	Anita Reeves
Tom Noone	John Olohan
Mary Quirke	Maureen Potter
John Turney	John Kavanagh
Karl/Carlos	Luke Griffin
Madeleine	Antoine Byrne
Colleen/Ingrid	Marion O'Dwyer

Directed by **Joe Dowling**
Designed by **Frank Conway**
Lighting by **Trevor Dawson**

CHARACTERS

Removals Man
His Assistant
Ellie Noone
Tom Noone
Mary Quirke, Ellie's mother
John Turvey
Karl/Carlos, the Noones' son
Madeleine, the Noones' daughter
Colleen, Ellie's sister (1957)
Ingrid, Ellie's sister (1987)

The action takes place in a small town near Dublin

Part One: 14 Martello Road; Friday, 12th July, 1957

Part Two: 14 Martello Lawn; Saturday, 11th July, 1987

Author's Note: Although there is a 30 year gap between the two parts of the play, the characters do not age in the slightest. These are basically the same people and at the same age

Other plays by Hugh Leonard
published by Samuel French Ltd:

Da
A Life
Mick and Mick
Patrick Pearse Motel
Pizzazz: *containing*
A View From the Obelisk
Roman Fever
Pizzazz
The Poker Session
Summer
Suburb of Babylon: *containing*
A Time of Wolves and Tigers
Nothing Personal
Last of the Last of the Mohicans

PART ONE

The stage is utterly bare except for a mountain of household effects covered by a dust-sheet. To one side of this there are two tea-chests; one contains books, draughtboard, Monopoly, portable radio—the stuff of leisure; the other has chinaware, bric-a-brac and ornaments, each piece wrapped in newspaper. Before the play begins, the Removals Man and his young Assistant enter carrying a sofa between them. The Removals Man considers, then directs the Assistant where it should be placed. Then, between them, they remove the dust cover revealing fireside chairs, a table, sideboard, standard lamp and whatever else belongs in the living room

At this point the Stage Lights begin to come up so that the disposal of the furniture becomes an overture to the play, with the Removals Man directing the operation. When all is in position, the House Lights go down

Removals Man (*with a flourish*) Now!

Now he and his Assistant supervize the erection of the house itself. A few pieces are flown in and guided into position by the two men. There should be no attempt at realism, only a suggestion of boundaries and of the kind of house it is: Number 14, Martello Road, a terrace house with a pocket-handkerchief front garden. We see this garden, a hallway, the beginnings of stairs, and the living room. It is all done very quickly. The Removals Man looks off anxiously past the garden, then calls to the flies:

Front door, if you please, soon as ever.

The front door flies into position

And not a second too . . .

He goes quickly to the door, just in time to open it for Ellie Noone. She is thirty-nine and conscious that she should behave as befits a woman who is moving towards middle-age. The foolishness of youth has been put away like a frock that is no longer becoming. She is dressed plainly and yet is careful of her appearance. She is carrying a pile of bed linen

Ma'am, are you mad, allow me. (*To his Assistant*) Eamonn, be useful. (*He takes the bed-linen from Ellie and give it to his Assistant*) There we go. Mrs Noone, ma'am, if I may be so forward . . .

Ellie Excuse me?

Removals Man . . . as to bid you a hearty welcome to the new abode.

Ellie (*shyly*) Thanks very much. (*She sees that the furniture is in place*) Oh, everything has been . . .

Removals Man All in its place, says I, and all in the wrong place, says you. (*As an afterthought*) Oh, and we put up the house for you.

Ellie (*politely*) Aren't you good.

Removals Man (*modestly*) Not at all, not a bit of it . . .

Ellie (*slightly nervous*) Weren't we steeped that the morning held? With it on the wireless that the good weather 'ud break, I thought what if the poor furniture gets lashed on?

Removals Man The twelfth of July, nineteen-fifty-seven, ma'm. A Friday. That day, it bucketed from four o'clock on. It was the end of the heatwave.

Ellie (*sorry to hear it*) Ah, no.

Removals Man It's not on the blow of three yet, so we're an hour to the good. Home . . . and dry.

Ellie (*looking wistfully at the room*) Still and all . . .

Removals Man Aha?

Ellie It's little enough there was to move. The way it all looks so small.

Removals Man Sure won't it grow?

Ellie (*amused*) Will it? How will it?

Removals Man (*grinning*) Same as children.

Ellie I can't see what call there was to go and move. Weren't we grand?

Removals Man A body can't stay still, ma'am.

Ellie (*unconvinced*) Can they not? I dunno.

Removals Man Else we'd be telling the same tale twice. Can't have that. And if nobody moved, him and me 'ud go broke. Think of it . . . no more Sunday night hops for Eamonn.

Ellie says something that is hardly audible, perhaps because the Removals Man is a stranger and the thought is treasonable

Excuse me?

Ellie I was saying the way people . . . the way they get above themselves.

Removals Man (*with charm*) Ma'am . . . physically impossible. Now will Eamonn take the stuff upstairs for you? Bedding. Is that it?

Ellie (*to the Assistant*) Thanks. I'll show you.

Removals Man I'll just make a start on the delph and the glasses.

This has the effect of detaining Ellie

Ellie (*shyly*) Excuse me, but how much did you say it . . . it would cost?

Removals Man Cost?

Ellie The price of the . . .

Removals Man Of the removal! I have you. The standard rate is by the hour. Seven and sixpence, by prior quotation to his good self.

Ellie For an hour. I see.

Removals Man Five of them gone already and another hour to unpack these fellas (*meaning the tea-chests*). That'll be a grand total of . . .

Ellie I was thinking . . . sure you needn't.

Removals Man Pardon me?

Ellie Needn't bother with the delph. I mean, we'll do it ourselves. (*Weakly*) It'll pass the evening for us.

He realizes that she wishes to save the extra hour's money. He is solicitous, careful that she should save face

I mean . . . (*she is tongue-tied*)

Removals Man You mean, it'd be all the same to you if we knocked off now?

She looks at him, helpless

Sure why don't we? Game ball, so. And if there is one aspect of the job I dislike, it is the breakables. (*Raising his palms*) See them, ma'am? Damp at the mere mention. Besides, you're the one who knows what goes where. Eamonn and me 'ud only be . . .

The Assistant coughs: a hint that the Removals Man is overdoing it

So we'll finish up and leave you to it. Eamonn . . .

Ellie I'll take the sheets. Mammy aired them for me. (*She takes the bedclothes, then starts uncertainly towards the kitchen*)

Removals Man (*pointing*) The stairs, ma'am? There's your road.

Ellie corrects her course and goes upstairs

(*To the Assistant*) Did I make a meal of it?

With a nod, the Assistant directs his attention to the audience

I know.

The Removal Man addresses us directly for the first time

This is the day the Noones forsook the old ways for the new. Time nudging and shoving them; them prodding time and nudging it. This is what they did and said the first hour of the first day. Nineteen fifty-seven, yes. July the twelfth. Orangeman's Day. Six babies born out of the town today; five of them Catholic. Five brand-new das not saying a word, but thinking what an inauspicious start the date was. The date has no significance for us, but. It's a day . . . (*with a shrug*) the end of the heat wave. *His* day.

He is referring to Tom Noone, who has appeared in the garden area. He has a brown paper bag, containing a six-pack, with him. Tom stands back looking at the house with an excitement that is barely containable

Him . . . (*Smiling*) Tom Noone. See him? Forty-two, going on seventeen. Him and old Mr Cussens run the grocer's on the Railway Road. It's called Cussens's, but Holmes is the name over the window . . . there was a time I knew why. He met herself—Ellie Quirke-that-was—at a dance at the White Cottage. Summer of nineteen thirty-five. She was with her sister.

Tom (*overhearing*) Her sister Colleen. Who died.

Removals Man Above in Peamount.

Tom Nineteen forty.

Removals Man T.B. was all the go in them days, same as polio is now. Colleen. Her ma named her after a one who used to be in the silent films.

Tom Colleen Moore. I never heard of her.

From upstairs, Ellie's voice is heard

Ellie (*off*) Tom, are you out there for the day?

Tom Two ticks.

Removals Man What's she at?

Tom Putting up curtains.

Removals Man Tom and Ellie were married in thirty-eight. Four children . . . eighteen, seventeen, twelve and seven . . . The twelve-year-old is off on the island with the sea scouts, and a neighbour—there'll be new neighbours after today—is minding the youngest. So the two small ones won't bother us. It is what is known as theatrical husbandry. There's a cat, too . . . it's off up the town. (*He goes to the door and addresses Tom*) 'Afternoon Mr N. Well wear, as they say.

Tom Isn't it great?

Removals Man Big day, what?

Tom (*modestly*) Ah, yeah.

Removals Man Great times we're living in. Would you say now we're on our feet at last?

Tom I thought, you know, a decent house 'ud give the kids a bit of a . . . a leg up.

Removals Man And yourselves.

Tom Yes. Well.

Removals Man What harm in that? Don't yous deserve it?

Tom I grew up in Darley's Lane, behind the tram-yard.

Removals Man Gone, now. Knew it well.

Tom How bad we were. If you lived out of the town, up by the quarry, like Ellie did, they'd swear to it you ate your young.

The Assistant sniggers

Removals Man (*to the Assistant*) Laugh away. It's true.

Tom When her and me were doing the . . . the thing, the steady line, like . . . we got the offer of what used to be the gate lodge above at Creebrishta . . . you know, where they pulled the old house down to build the nurseries. Four rooms, ten bob a week. Thought we were landed.

Removals Man And now!

Tom Yeah, a house with stairs in it. (*Laughing at himself*) God, I'm a eejit.

Removals Man Certainly stairs—and a bathroom at the head of them. What's eejity?

Tom Fair dues, it's herself we may thank. A powerful manager. Do you hear me?

This last to Ellie, who has appeared

Ellie You came in, then? I suppose you never thought of me ciggies?
Tom Don't be such an old grouse. When do I ever not think of them?
  Here. (*To the Removals Man*) Her allowance.

*He produces two cigarette packs; a half-empty one of "Capstan" or
"Players Navy Cut" for himself; for her, an unopened pack of cork-tips*

Ellie (*to the Removals Man*) I was gasping.

*Tom takes one from his own packet for himself, then offers one to the
Removals Man*

Tom Will you stick to the pipe?
Removals Man I never say no. G'luck.
Tom (*to the Assistant*) Yourself?
Assistant Ta. (*He takes one*)

*Tom lights his own cigarette and Ellie's. He makes to light the Removals
Man's, but from superstition the latter blows the match out and lights his
own. The Assistant comes forward and lights his off the Removals Man's
before the latter can take it from between his lips. All four begin to puff
contentedly, inhaling deeply. Clouds of smoke ascend. Silence for
twenty seconds*

Removals Man Well, it's knocking-off time. Eamonn, good lad, tidy
  up.

In his own time the Assistant folds up the dust sheet

Tom Excuse me, why is it . . .
Removals Man Mrs Noone, ah . . .
Ellie I thought we might as well unpack the rest ourselves, Tom. It's
  only the few bits.
Tom There's two . . .

*He is about to say that there are two tea chests to be unpacked but
breaks off, aware that the Removals Man can hear*

Ellie It's like Mr. . . .
Removals Man Mangan.
Ellie . . . Mr Mangan says. We know what goes where and he doesn't.
  Mammy'll help us, and the children can unpack their own stuff
  that's upstairs. Sure we'll be done in no time.
Removals Man (*to Tom*) Mrs N., never a truer word came out of you
  . . . a toppin' manager.

Tom (*embarrassed*) Yeah, great. (*Then, as a diversion*) Well, you're not leaving here without a drop of something to damp down the dust.

Tom takes from the brown paper bag a six-pack of stout. The Removals Man makes a great show of astonishment

Removals Man You what? What are you doing? Are you demented?
Tom You'll have just the one.
Removals Man Are you trying to destroy me? No. I will not.
Tom I say you will.
Removals Man And I say different.
Tom When it's offered, can't you take it like a Christian?
Removals Man I won't. Not if you were to go on your benders.
Tom You mean it?
Removals Man I do.
Tom (*affecting to give up*) Then the devil's cure to you.
Removals Man (*taking the bottle*) You're a hopeless bloody man. (*To Ellie*) I say, he's a shocker.

She smiles nervously

Tom Does your lad take e'er a . . .
Assistant Ta. (*He takes the proffered bottle*)
Removals Man (*seemingly ferocious*) What? You. Here. What do you think you're at? Come here, I say.

He advances on the Assistant, who cringes and makes to relinquish the bottle. Instead of taking it, the Removals Man produces an opener attached to his key ring and whips the cap off

There. (*A wink to Tom*) Outside, now. Don't be under people's feet. (*To Tom and Ellie, raising his bottle*) G'luck.

He and the Assistant go out into the garden. They sit on an empty packing case.

Tom What did you say to him?
Ellie When?
Tom I booked him for the full day.
Ellie Now you're going to be cross.
Tom I'm not cross.
Ellie Well for you, then, for you've no right to be. What I done, I saved us money.

Tom Oh, sure, and by tomorrow the town'll have it that we were too mean to spend five shillings.

Ellie Seven-and-six.

Tom (*mock horror*) What? Oh, my God, seven shillings and sixpence!

Ellie Shh. (*She glances towards the garden*) Jeer all you want. Yes, seven and sixpence, and at the rate you're going it won't be long before you'll folly a crow for it.

Tom Ellie, we spent so much, and now, all for the sake of a measly few . . .

Ellie We spent *too* bloomin' much. You have me frightened the way the divil's run off with you. Look at the sticks of furniture. They're lost because the house is too big for them.

Tom Not at all.

Ellie It's true. We were grand where we were.

Tom A body has to spread his wings.

Ellie (*almost smiling*) Wings? Us?

Tom The old house . . .

Ellie What?

Tom It was too . . .

Ellie "Old house"! My God and us not an hour out of it.

Tom It wasn't a credit to us.

Ellie If you can say that, you have no nature. 'Twas so a credit to us. I had it like a new pin. Anyone could walk in, morning or night, and now all you can do is belittle it.

Tom I never be . . .

Ellie Yes, you do. Giving out to me for saving us a few . . .

Tom I never gave out. I said, for the sake of seven shillings and . . .

Ellie Always wanting to chop and change, like as if there was a . . . a bee in you. Oh, that day you came home and said it was goodbye to Creebrishta. With a smile on you as if it was a present you had for us. To leave a place where I could wake up in the morning and didn't need to open my eyes to know what was around me or where I was. Now I don't know an'thin'.

Tom Be fair. Give it time.

Ellie (*with pride*) I won't. Doesn't deserve time.

Tom Then I give up.

Ellie You? Give up? Catch you!

Tom (*laughing*) You're a right old misery . . . afraid to throw a shadow in case it snaps back at you. God, when I was a kid I used to look at my ma and dad, making a living, putting a home together, rearing us. I'd wonder: when I grow up will the world move over for me to find a place in it? Will I be worth my salt, same as them? And the time came. I left school. I got the job, I met you, and there was nothing to it. It was a snip. I thought maybe we could mark time and be glad of it, keep our heads down. Stay out of the wet. Instead, we're on the move.

Ellie (*bitterly*) Don't I know!

Tom Love, wherever we end up, seven and a kick won't make much difference.

In the garden, the Removals Man and his Assistant are enjoying their stout

Removals Man Did you know, Eamonn, that a week from tomorrow, over in the town of Bedford in Limeyland, old MacMillan is going to get up and say that the people have never had it so good?

Assistant That so?

Removals Man (*a nod towards Tom*) Remember you heard it here first.

Tom Pity of it is, love, you did that poor man out of his day's money.

Ellie How? When did I?

Tom Gone a bit late in the day for him to make it up.

Ellie (*in dismay*) Is it? Oh, Tommy, I never thought.

Tom He won't forget you in a hurry.

Ellie Oh, my God, his poor wife. What'll he say to her?

Tom There goes her fur coat.

Ellie Shut up. You're not to. I ought to have held me tongue. (*As an admission*) I got afraid.

Tom So will we make it up to him?

Ellie How?

Tom Will we tell him to unpack the tea-chests?

Ellie (*humbly*) No. No, I told him not to. It 'ud shame me.

Tom Well then, how about if I make it up to him . . . pay him his seven-and-sixpence? All right?

She wrestles with her frugality

Ellie Do you mean . . . for doing nothing?

Tom (*mock-serious*) Dead right. Five bob, then?

She is defeated. She nods unhappily, unwillingly. Tom takes hold of her in a wave of affection

Tom You're a marvellous bloody woman, do you know that?

He hugs her and attempts to kiss her. She resists, not because she is cold-natured, but because of upbringing. It is unseemly; the rites of courtship are done with

Ellie What are you doing?
Tom It's a great day for us.
Ellie For you it is. (*Breaking free, almost hissing*) Tom, we're not in a fillum! (*She goes to one of the tea-chests and makes a show of unpacking various small articles, each of which is wrapped in newspaper*)

Mrs Mary Quirke appears in the garden. She is sixty-four and looks it; not a year more, not a day less. On the surface she is vulnerable, one of life's unprotesting victims; underneath, there is a quite ruthless determination to prevail on her own terms. Under her arm she carries two framed photographs; one is of her daughter Colleen, taken in the late '30s; the other is Mary's own wedding picture, taken with her bridegroom, Jem Quirke, in nineteen-fifteen. She is at the moment in mellow mood

Removals Man 'Afternoon, Mrs Quirke. Do you not remember me?
Mary I'm not doting yet. It's Martin Mangan.
Removals Man You have a great memory.
Mary What odds if I hadn't? I seen the oul' horse.
Tom (*looking out*) It's your mother.
Ellie (*a hint of concern*) How is she?
Tom Grand.
Mary Didn't the day hold up for us? (*Quietly, firmly*) Yes . . . yes, it did. (*It is her manner to reassert what she says, as if refuting a suggestion to the contrary*)
Removals Man (*indicating the house*) So what do you think?
Mary God send them good luck in it. And they'll have it . . . yes, they will.
Removals Man And yourself. Won't you be in it with them?
Mary I daresay. For the little time that's left.
Removals Man Now sing another come-all-you. You'll see the lot of us out.
Mary I've had me day.
Removals Man When was that, then?

Mary What? Ah, the town's gone different, the old characters dead and gone. No one singing the tunes any more. Look. Look up there. (*She points up, away from the house*)

Removals Man What's that, then?

Mary Television sets.

The action of pointing, together with the few drinks she has had, causes the pictures to slither from her arm. The Removals Man catches them

Removals Man Careful, ma'am. You don't want to break your pictures.

Mary You never spoke truer word, for me heart 'ud go with them. No furniture van for these.

Ellie Tom, be useful. Give me a hand.

Tom (*who has seen the near-accident*) She . . . (*He thinks better of speaking and instead moves to help her with the unpacking*)

Mary This one, look. That's Jem Quirke the day him and me was married . . . when was it? Jem be name and gem be nature. Have you me?

Removals Man (*soberly*) Oh, I do.

Mary No better man trod shoe leather. He was a trooper. And this is my Colleen that's . . . that's gone. (*She is suddenly in tears*) Jesus, why is it always the best that's took? Answer me.

Ellie (*to Tom*) What's she doing?

Removals Man Now haven't you a great girl inside? The best in the world. Amn't I right?

Mary nods sullenly

You know I am.

Mary (*ungiving*) Colleen was the bestest. (*Pause*) Hold these for me. If she sees I've a drop took she'll give out to me. She has no nature. (*She gives the pictures to the Removals Man, fishes in her bag for a handkerchief and sets about making herself presentable. She is making conversation*) So the time Jem and me was married—me brain is addled . . . what year was it . . .?

The Removals Man makes a motion to his Assistant, who takes a notebook from his apron pocket

No matter. Tell me this and tell me no more, was it yourself or your da that moved us into The Dwellin's?

Removals Man Couldn't have been me, ma'am.

Assistant (*reading*) "Married nineteen-seventeen."

Removals Man Before my time.

Assistant (*reading*) "Jem Quirke, born eighteen-ninety-one, died nineteen-thirty of typhoid."

Removals Man An unusual ailment for the time.

Assistant He got a good offer. Five shillings to clear a drain that was blocked. Couldn't say no to that. (*Reading*) Herself will pop off the second of May, nineteen-seventy.

Removals Man You have no head for drink . . .

Assistant Of a stroke.

Removals Man I said, that'll do you. (*Restoring the pictures to Mary*) You're right as rain now, ma'am. In you go.

Mary Thanks. Thanks. (*She goes into the house*) So are we settled in?

Ellie Mammy, where were you?

Mary We are . . . yes, we are, aren't we grand? How bad we are.

Ellie Ah, Mammy, the cut of you.

Mary What cut?

Ellie turns away from her with impatience, venting her annoyance on the unpacking of objects. Mary's malice begins to stir

Oh, I see . . . yes I do. I'm not to be let say goodbye to me old neighbours. No matter all the good turns that Mag Tynan done for me.

Ellie Excuse me. Saying goodbye to who, did you say?

Tom Ellie, leave go of it.

Ellie Mrs Tynan lives a stone's throw from here. She'll be nearer to you now than she ever was.

Mary Out of her heart's goodness, the woman offered me a drink. For the day that was in it. The once in a blue moon.

Ellie Oh yes, the day that's in it. Like Christmas Day and New Year's and Easter and Whit and the first Monday in August. I can't even look at the sky but there's a blue moon in it.

Mary (*under her breath*) Faggot.

Ellie Mammy, you know that when you have a sup took it goes back on you.

Mary It's not the sup that goes back on me. People go back on me. 'S no matter. (*With a show of rising above pettiness of mind, she takes up one of the pages of newspaper that was used for wrapping. She sits on the sofa and opens the paper with a flourish, not noticing that it is yellow with age*) Might as well see what's happening in the world.

She affects to read. Ellie darts an angry look at her and goes on with the unpacking. Tom takes another two bottles of stout from the bag. He passes Ellie on his way out

Tom (*in an aside*) She's not too bad. Let it lie. (*He goes out into the garden and proffers the bottles to the Removals Man*)

Removals Man Blessings on you. (*Refusing the second bottle*) What? No . . . not for him. Smell of a cork and he's gone. (*He indicates firmly that the Assistant is not to be given a second bottle*)

Tom Bad luck to take it back. (*He leaves the second bottle and goes back inside*)

Removals Man (*with affected annoyance*) You're a hopeless bloody man.

Mary Oh, Mother of God.

Tom and Ellie stare at her. She is holding the paper open

Tom What's up?

Mary There's one of them airships gone and crashed.

Ellie One of them what?

Mary (*ignoring her*) Did you see that, Tommy?

Tom Sorry?

Mary (*reading laboriously, broken pince-nez in position*) "The Tragic Fate of the R101. Famed British Airship Crashes in France." It's true, it's true, we know not the day nor the hour.

Ellie Mammy, what are you . . .

Tom whispers to her, explaining. Ellie looks at the paper, which is the "Dublin Evening Mail", then quickly turns her back on Mary, but cannot stifle a hiccuping whimper of laughter. It is infectious; Tom and Ellie kneel over the tea-chests, their shoulders heaving

Mary (*looking at them*) Oh ay, that's the Irish people for you. They'll cry their eyes out for foreigners, but not their own.

Ellie Mammy, that paper is . . .

Tom makes to silence her

John Turvey appears outside. He carries a largish parcel; obviously it is a wall picture. He is a year younger than Tom; tweed jacket with leather elbow patches; a fountain pen and two ballpoints showing in his breast pocket; a gold fainne in his lapel. With him is Karl Noone, aged 18. He carries a French grammar and a notebook

John (*to the Removals Man*) Good day to you. (*Calling into the house*) Is there anyone in residence?

Removals Man (*almost deferential*) That's a fine day, sir.

Tom John's here . . . would you doubt him? (*Calling*) Good man, come on in.

Tom and Ellie are happy to have this visitor. The Removals Man puts a hand on John's shoulder, detaining him.

Removals Man (*to John*) Excuse me. (*To us*) Mr Turvey is a teacher at Harold Boys' School on the Bus Lawn. Butty of Tom Noone's ever since they were kids. Sound man, no codology.

John smiles modestly

And up to two years ago, this young gentleman was a pupil of his. Rotten with brains, and now, sign's on it, he's at the tech. He's their eldest, name of . . . ah . . .

Karl Karl. With a "K".

Karl and John move into the house area

Removals Man Karl with a "K". A month or so ago, it was Carl with a "C". Before that, it was plain Charles or Charlie or Chas. Now God alone knows where he's heading.

John Bail o Dhia ar an obair. How are you, Ellie, apart from having married the wrong man?

Ellie John, you're fierce.

John Eat you, so I would. And look who I met getting off his bus.

Karl 'Lo, mam . . . 'lo, dad.

Ellie Charlie, what brought you home? It isn't your time.

Karl I told Mr Gleason we were moving, and he thought I might be needed here to . . . (*he hesitates*)

John To help your parents, is that it? Ha-ha, and now you'll have to. Hoist with your own petard.

Tom (*indicating Mary*) Hey, John . . .

John Uh-huh. Cathal, what was it you said?

Removals Man Cathal! Where will it end?

John You were let off? Have you a holiday job?

Ellie No. Mr Gleason is giving him a . . . a . . .

Karl A grind.

Tom John . . . look.

John What? Mrs Quirke, I didn't see a bit of you. Are you well?

Mary Grand. Not a feather out of me.

Tom Mrs Quirke was reading to us about the crash of the R101.

John Oh, yes?

Tom In the paper.

John *Was* she? Well, now!

Ellie Don't start, the pair of you.

John (*stooping to read the reverse*) And oh, my God, the rebels have seized the G.P.O.!

Mary When?

John "General Pearse reads Proclamation."

Mary (*turning the paper*) Where?

Karl Granny, they're having you on. There hasn't been an "Evening Mail" these donkey's years. (*He mispronounces "donkey"*)

Mary Hasn't been a what?

John (*pleasantly*) Not "dunkey", Cathal. It's "donkey".

Perhaps John is rapping Karl for spoiling the joke; or perhaps what he says is from pedagogic force of habit. On Karl's part, there is the constraint of a schoolboy towards his natural enemy, and he replies as a schoolboy would, accepting the rebuke and resenting it

Karl Yes, sir.

Mary Well, divil's cure to yous.

Ellie Mammy, it was a joke.

Mary 'Twasn't. It was a jeer. I'm going to hang up me pictures.

Ellie Do. Then come back down and we'll have a cup of tea. Seeing as we're here and there's no help for it, we might as well.

John Yes, well, I'll be out of the way. (*He picks up his parcel*) The reason I . . .

Tom You'll stay here.

John No, I won't.

Tom For a cup in your hand.

John No.

Tom Yes.

John Can't, honestly. I have to be . . .

Tom Five minutes. Can you not . . .

Ellie (*exploding*) For God's sake, we've been through this with the removals man. "You'll have a jar?" "I won't have a jar." "You will have a jar." "I won't have a jar." "You will." "I won't." (*To John*) Now Jesus, sit and have a feckin' cup of tea! (*Then, embarrassed by her outburst*) Excuse me. I'll put the kettle on.

Ellie exits

Mary That was lovely.

Mary goes upstairs

Karl (*wanting to ease out*) Yeah . . . well . . .
John Cathal, I oughtn't to have corrected you. Sorry.

Karl nods curtly

Tom Son, what do you say?
John (*to Karl*) The curse of being a schoolmaster is you talk at people
    instead of to them. So ignore me, OK? Cathal?
Tom Well, answer him.
Karl He said to ignore him.
Tom You what?

*Tom lashes out at Karl. It is a clumsy and half-hearted slap, and Karl
avoids it easily by taking a pace back*

John Hey, whoa there . . . easy.
Tom You little bowsie. Lucky for you your mother is out of the
    room.
John Tom, it was . . .
Tom She'd bloody crease him.
John It was a joke. Cathal took me at my word. More power to him.
Tom A joke?
John (*to Karl*) Certainly, a joke. Best of friends, what?
Karl (*as Tom looks at him*) Yes, sir.
John Tom, do you hear him? "Sir"! Thinks he's still at Harold Boys!
    (*To Karl*) Cathal, the "sir" days are over. You know my name.
Tom John.
John Or, if that sticks in his craw, "Mr Turvey." Anything for God's
    sake except "Sir". Or "Topsy".
Karl You what?
John Come on! You think I don't know my own nickname? What
    else would you call a teacher who had the misfortune to be a
    Turvey?
Karl We never thought you knew.
John You thick, you. I knew the first day I set foot in Harold Boys'.
Tom Topsy, what?
John You dry up.

Karl Excuse me. Since we're on the subject of names, would you . . .
John Well?
Karl Would you mind not calling me Cathal?
John Oh?
Karl Because nobody else does.
John Good Irish name. (*Yielding*) Grand. So what's your preference?
Tom We call him Charlie.
Karl (*overlapping*) My name's Karl.
Tom Oh yeah, I forgot. Karl. Kids today . . . at school, how do you not murder them?
John Be thankful. If it's not Cathal, at least it's not . . . (*very British*) . . . Chawrrles. So, Karl—said he, giving it a trial run—what's this grind of yours?
Karl I'm doing French.
John Well, now!
Tom (*proudly*) Far from it he was reared, says you.
Karl For quantity surveying, you need an extra language.
John I see. What about Irish?
Karl We have to have that. It's compulsory.
John What if it wasn't? Say it was optional. Would you go for it?

Karl shrugs, unwilling to answer and resenting the question

John (*with a smile, meaning the opposite*) I'm sure you would!

Ellie appears

Ellie Charlie, go and wash your hands.

Karl moves towards her

Not in the kitchen . . . upstairs. (*With a look at Tom*) There's a bathroom now. And tell your granny the tea is near ready.

Karl goes upstairs, glad to make his escape

As Ellie is about to return to the kitchen

Tom Ellie, could we not wait until Madeleine comes in?
Ellie What for? She'll get her proper tea at six, same as the rest of us.
Tom I know, yes. I thought it would be nice if we had our first cup of tea in the new house . . . I mean her and Karl and you and me. All of us.
Ellie What age are you?

Ellie goes out into the kitchen

Tom Ellie has no sense of occasion. I think it's nice to be together. Sort of you go shares, and later on you can say "Hey . . . hey, remember that day?" You know?

John You press it in the book?

Tom Pardon?

John The book. The album.

Tom Yeah! Good man.

John So where's Madeleine, then?

Tom Off hitting some ball some place. We didn't want her to get trampled on in the general frenzy.

John Your removals men aren't exactly what you'd call streaks of lightning, are they?

Tom Sore point, John, don't scratch it. (*He puts a finger to his lips and points with the other hand towards the kitchen*)

John Oh. (*Pause*) Tom, while we're on our ownsome . . .

Tom Have a jar.

John (*declining*) . . . I don't know if you've noticed, but Cathal . . . Karl . . . whatever he calls himself, he and I don't hit it off. Never have done.

Tom (*after a moment, bluntly*) Why is that?

John What you're supposed to say is: "John, are you mad? The lad thinks the sun shines out of you."

Tom (*stolidly*) He doesn't.

John No. Tom, it's in the diplomatic corps you should have been.

Tom Say your say . . . I hear cups.

John So why I bring it up now is because on top of all else, I don't want him to take me for an informer.

Tom I see. You're going to spoil today on me, aren't you?

John Of a Sunday, what Mass does Cathal go to?

Tom The half-eleven. Ellie gives him a shilling for the plate.

John Thought so. I go to the ten o'clock. Then I take the dog for a walk down the pier. And that's where Cathal is, hanging around the bandstand.

Tom Cathal? (*Amending*) Charlie?

John Every Sunday the same gang. Fellows and young ones . . . girls. He thinks I don't see him.

Tom Girls.

John Talking, that's all. Nice kids. Well-dressed. You know . . .
Sunday clothes.

Tom Clothes for missing Mass in.

John It was a conundrum. I thought do I mind my own interference?
Or do I carry tales on him to you?

Tom Which did you decide?

John (*smarting*) I didn't expect to be thanked. It was a choice
between . . .

Tom I know, I know. We're mates.

John And I'm aware that you hold fast to certain ideas. About the
family.

Tom Well, why not? Always have done. What I insist on . . .
(*Probably it is his first time to put it into words*) . . . there's to be
nothing that can't be said straight out. I mean, by the kids to us,
and by us to them.

John A tall order.

Tom (*a hard-liner*) Maybe.

John Yes. So will you tell Ellie? About Cathal.

Tom Jesus, no, she'd eat him. Still, if he's missing Mass and not
telling me, there must be something radically . . .

*As Ellie comes in with a tray on which there are tea things and a plate
of buttered brack, Tom changes the subject*

. . . radically different from my day. The time I was at school, we
had a baldy old divil we nicknamed Tabac. (*In a murderous voice*)
"The horse latitudes are in Punchestown, do you tell me? Get out
here to me, you mongrel's melt."

Ellie (*mildly*) Tom, we're going to eat.

John Punchestown? That's a yarn. No one answered him that.

Tom Didn't they? I got six, three on each hand.

Ellie goes to the stairs

Ellie Mammy . . . Charlie . . . will the pair of you come . . . Oh, there
yous are.

Mary and Karl appear

Now it's rough and ready, the way you see it. Sit where you can and
don't wait to be asked. Charlie . . . move a chair for your
grandmother.

Karl She took Madeleine's room.

Ellie Who's "she"? The cat's aunt? Sit and be quiet.

Karl Dad, Granny took . . .

Tom I'll talk to you later.

Karl Why? What did I do?

Ellie Sit!

John (*moving to go*) Look, this is for family. I promised my landlady I'd . . .

Tom No, you did not. The policy of this house is to provide food for the hungry and a roof for the homeless. So shush.

John, Karl and Mary sit, Mary still nursing her grievance. There is the business of pouring the tea and passing the slices of brack. Tom smiles upon it all, filled with the sense of the occasion. The Removals Man is watching him

Removals Man The sun is shining out of him. If he could, he'd put it on the wireless.

He sees that the Assistant is looking in the other direction

What are you gawking at?

Assistant Nothing.

Removals Man You're on the look-out for the young one.

Assistant No, I'm not. What young one?

Removals Man Madeleine. Young Maddie.

Assistant (*he smiles at the name, then*) Who?

Ellie (*with mock severity*) If John is homeless, he has only himself to blame. No wife at his age, and neither chick nor child. A nice example for the boys under him.

John Ellie, I loved a girl once, and she went and wed another.

Ellie You never did. When?

John You know her well.

Ellie Go 'way. Who was she?

John blows Ellie a kiss

Oh, you brat.

Tom Ellie is right. You haven't a proper home, you own nothing. God, even the old dog you walk on Sundays is your landlady's.

John I have no wish to own things. As for marrying, I simply haven't met the . . .

Tom . . . right girl yet.

Ellie Don't be so particular. There's dozens of nice girls. Any of them
'ud be a credit to you, and not a pick of differ between one and the
next.

Tom Pardon me?

Ellie (*to John*) Men only pretend that there is.

Tom What?

Ellie A difference.

Tom (*staring at her*) God almighty you'd think they were eggs in an
eggbox.

Ellie (*ignoring him; to John*) You'll have a family and a nice home and
be safe.

John Will I? And what about the pram in the hall?

Ellie What pram?

John Figure of speech. Cyril Connolly, an English writer, says that
the artist's worst enemy is the pram in the hall.

Tom Are you an artist, then? Since when.

Karl Yeah, thatched cottages.

Tom jabs a finger at him in anger

Tom (*a threat*) You! Shut it!

John I mean, I want to play my part in helping us to hold on to what's
ours. To be sure, all of us have to go forward, same as you today. It
can't be stopped, but that doesn't mean we're obliged to forget
where we've been or leave behind what makes us different from the
rest. We have baggage to take with us.

Karl mumbles

Speak up.

Karl I said, like speaking Irish?

John Yes, Irish, why not? Or English, even, as long as it hasn't been
abused and kicked around. I mean . . . it's Karl at the moment,
isn't it? . . . what I mean, Karl, is that you have your kind of family,
and I have mine.

Mary Your ma and da, yes.

Tom No, they're both . . .

John (*over-riding him*) Yes, yes, my mam and dad, why not? (*To
Mary*) Well said. Because for good or ill, my parents—and by the
way, there are thousands of them—are like no one else's that were
ever born, or ever will be. So I'll not see them thrown into a great
melting pot where we all step it out to the same tune and the life we

live is in a currency that's not our own. I want to help us hold on to
what we are . . . with a book or a play, maybe, or even politics.
Whatever I'm fit for. We've been the world's blotting paper long
enough. (*To Mary again*) Don't mind me, ma'am. I got ahead of
myself.

Mary I kep' up with you.

John (*mildly surprised*) Did you? Good woman, so.

Ellie (*after a moment of unease*) Well, what I say is, could you be up to
him? A wife would be a *help* to you.

John And children?

Ellie Certainly, children!

Tom No, John is like in *Goodbye, Mr Chips*.

John Who's that, then?

Tom You know, in the film. Oh, come on.

John shakes his head

He's the old schoolteacher . . . you know? And he's dying. And the
doctor says what a pity he never had any children. And Mr Chips
hears him, and he says . . . "You're wrong, you know. I have so
had children, thousands of them . . ."

Tom ⎫
Karl ⎭ (*together*) . . . all boys"!

*Tom laughs delighted at Karl being in tune with him, then scowls,
remembering that Karl is out of favour*

John That's good. "All boys." Ha-ha.

Karl (*to Tom*) What's up?

John Yes, I like that.

Mary (*suddenly*) They ought to bring back the trams.

Tom What?

Mary The man is right, so he is. Everything now is chop and change.
The old stock is all gone . . . yes, they are.

Ellie Mammy, people can't live forever.

Mary They can't, no and well for them. In their day, there was the big
houses with walls you couldn't see over and there was the cottages,
like in the Square or The Dwellin's. And there was nothin' in
between . . . no, there was not, no people who'd give you the sick
because they didn't know who the hell they were or where they
belonged. Now it's all noise and newness. Time in this town a body
could walk off of a footpath and be safe. Now go and look out of

that window. Three motor cars on a road the like of this. It's
scandalous.
Ellie I'll give Mammy that. She's right.
Mary Motor cars and the smell of them. The war was the only time
we had peace.
Tom (*sensing Ellie's antagonism*) I say, anyone that owns a car, more
power to him.
Mary Noise that'd deafen you and smoke that'd choke you. Today, I
cem round by McConkey's field that was. Ah, when I saw it. All
gone into gardens that a blade of grass 'ud be ashamed of. And
music coming out of the windows. Them and their scuffle.
Karl Skiffle.
Mary (*to John*) Y'ought to write a book to bring back the trams.
John It wasn't quite trams I had in mind, Mrs Quirke.
Tom Why not? I mean, who decides what's to be kept and what isn't?
John The one who tries hardest.
Ellie Charlie, give me over your cup . . . (*She replenishes his cup*)

*In the garden, the Removals Man, without looking towards the road,
knows that Madeleine is close by*

Removals Man She's here now.
Assistant (*with affected innocence*) Who is?
Removals Man Young Madeleine. Mad for short. (*To us*) She's the
seventeen-year-old.

*Madeleine appears, carrying a patched-up tennis racquet. She is a
pretty girl. She stops at the front gate and waves goodbye to a friend
with a gesture that is oddly formal without being overdone*

The Assistant cannot take his eyes from her

You would not think it to look at her, but at this moment she is
Audrey Hepburn, and tomorrow is her coronation.

*Her leave-taking done, Madeleine folds her cardigan across her breast
as if it were an evening wrap. She smiles in recollection*

Not tomorrow . . . today. It's gone four in the morning, and she
has been out mixing with the common people, unbeknownst. This
is the summer Madeleine began, when she left off sitting on walls
and being only a young one. How is it, Maddie? I suppose I might
as soon ask a hawthorn what the month of May is like?
Madeleine (*shyly, smiling*) It's lovely.

She turns to enter the house, but is brought up short on finding that the Assistant has summoned up the courage to stand in her path

Assistant Hello.
Madeleine 'lo.

She is confused and a little frightened, not knowing how to handle the situation. The Assistant finds himself tongue-tied with embarrassment. He simply stares at her. She takes a step to her right to outflank him; he counters by stepping to his left

Removals Man (*warningly*) Eamonn.

Madeleine steps back; so does the Assistant, still facing her. She steps to her left; he moves to his right

Eamonn . . . the girl isn't let go to dances.

Madeleine ducks past the Assistant, enters the house and pauses for a moment to regain her composure. The Removals Man frowns.

Son, don't do that again. We're working for them. They pay us. Know your place.

Madeleine comes into the living area

Madeleine Oh . . . you're having tea.
Tom Maddie . . . good girl. Now we can come to order. All together like Brown's cows, what?
John How are you, Madeleine?
Madeleine Hello, John. Hi, Karl.
Karl Hi, Mad.
Tom So what do you think of your new abode? Ellie, pour her a cup of tea.
Madeleine It's fab. No, I mean it, it's great. The time we came to see it, I thought this room was weenchy. Now it's big.
John That's the furniture.
Madeleine Get away.

Ellie offers her a teacup

In a minute, mam. I want to see what my room looks like. I can't wait.
Ellie Come back here . . . now, I say, and get that down you. And the pair of you, after you've had your proper tea at six o'clock, I want

you to unpack your clothes and books and whatever else is upstairs and put them away.

Karl I'll do mine tomorrow.

Ellie Excuse me, you'll do it this evening.

Karl Can't. I'm going to the pictures.

Tom What?

Karl I promised the lads.

Tom The lads . . . short for "ladies", is that it?

Karl (*smiling, incredulous*) Ah, come on.

Tom And who says you're going to be *let* go to the pictures?

Karl I'll do the room tomorrow. Where's the difference?

Madeleine (*gasping as she drinks*) Jesus.

Ellie Madeleine!

Madeleine I can't help it, I'm scalded.

Ellie Drink slower.

Karl God, it's like living in Russia. The stuff in the room is not going to run away.

Tom Are you answering back?

Ellie Tom, not a row on top of all else. Let him go to his old pictures.

Tom Oh, thanks. You started it; now you bail out.

Ellie I'm getting a headache with the pair of you.

Karl (*to Tom*) You're in a right friggin' wax today. What's up?

Tom I'm what? What did you say?

Incensed, Tom goes for Karl, hand raised. Karl slips out of range, then points a finger at Tom

Karl Don't . . . hit me.

Tom "Please".

Karl Please.

Tom That's better. (*His temper has expired as quickly as it flared up. He is glad to escape from the situation*)

Ellie 'Clare to God, one minute he has them spoiled, and the next he's trying to kill them. John, we're off to a great start.

John I'm neutral.

Tom (*part belief, part bluster*) The family may be going to hell elsewhere, but not here . . . not in this house, not yet.

Mary In my young day, it wasn't a slap we were gev. We got it hot and heavy with a shut fist.

Karl So can I go to the pictures?

John (*almost to himself, a reflex*) *May* I?

Mary Now we're too soft with them, and sign's on it they'd hang you.
Tom (*still sueing for peace*) We'll see.
Madeleine Mam, if the war's over can I go up and look at my room?
John (*to Karl*) So what's this film that's so unmissable?
Ellie He'd go to anything. He's picture-mad.
Madeleine (*thinking she has been called*) Hello.
Ellie No one's calling you. Go, if you're going.

  Madeleine goes upstairs

John What's the name of it?
Karl I dunno.
Tom Yes, you do know. Tell us.
Karl (*reluctantly*) It's called *She's Working Her Way Through College*.
John (*in disgust*) It's what? Cathal, you can't possibly. It's trash . . . utter rubbish.
Karl You haven't seen it.
John I don't have to see it.
Karl I think you do.
John My dear man, you hardly need to have been on Calvary to be a Catholic. The title tells me what it is. My God to sit for two hours in the dark listening to moronic drivel.
Tom Well, as long as there's nothing actually *wrong* with it . . .
Ellie . . . That's the main thing.
John Are you both quite mad? Or do my own senses make mock of me?
Tom John, it's the holliers, you're not in the schoolroom. (*To Karl, keeping the peace*) So . . . who's working her way through the college?
Karl What? Virginia Mayo.
John An Irish girl. At least that's something.
Mary My Colleen, God rest her, was called after an Irish girl that used to be on the films.
Ellie She wasn't Irish, Mammy.
Mary Excuse me, but she was.
Ellie You told me yourself that the priest nearly wouldn't do the christening on account of he said there was never a St. Colleen.
Mary She was called after a . . .
Ellie . . . after some American one that made up the name. Charlie found it out for me in one of his books.

Karl It's true. Her real name was . . .

Mary I won't listen. (*To Ellie*) Her name's all that's left of her, and you even begrudge her that.

Ellie All I'm saying is that the person you called her after . . .

Madeleine returns, distressed

Madeleine Mam . . . Granny went and took my room.

Ellie She done what?

Karl I told you. No one listens to me.

Madeleine Her clothes and her bedspread and the pictures of Aunt Colleen and Grandad are all in the room you said I was to have.

Ellie (*wearily*) Mammy, is this true?

Mary Sure I know Madeleine wouldn't say no to me. (*To Madeleine*) Weren't you always my favourite?

Madeleine Granny, come off it. You'd live in one of my ears and let the other one out in flats.

Ellie Madeleine, hold your tongue. Mammy, you can't have that room. Tom, tell her.

Tom Well, if she's so . . .

Ellie I say no. Madeleine and Dympna have to go halves, the same as Charlie and Ciaran, and I'm not putting them in a room they can't turn round in. (*She starts to go out*)

Tom Where are you going?

Ellie Where do you think? (*To Mary*) Have you nothing to do but make work for me?

Madeleine (*still angry*) Granny, the boldness of you. Grab, grab, grab.

Tom Madeleine, shush.

Madeleine No, honestly, she'd steal the willow pattern off a plate.

Mary A body is entitled to her bit of comfort, yes, she is.

Madeleine What about *our* bit of comfort?

Mary A room of her own where she's out of people's way . . . just to sit quiet and look out at the chapel.

Madeleine You can't see the church from that room.

Mary (*snapping*) You can see the roof! The young is selfish and always will be. *Yous* have tomorra and the next day and the day after, all of them different. What have I got? Not as many special days in a year as 'ud make a fortnight. There's the First Fridays and the holy days and the week of retreat, and before you can get up off your knees it's "Any apples or nuts?" and "How did you get over the Christmas?" Yous can laugh . . . it'll come to yous.

Tom You're a right misery. Haven't you your week in Skerries?
Mary (*implacable*) The sea is the sea.

There is a dragging noise from upstairs

Jesus, what's she pulling and hauling at? (*She begins to exit*) There's not one of yous'd give a body ditch.

Mary exits

Madeleine (*almost in mime*) Ditch?
Karl Ditch-water.
Tom Madeleine, you're very hard on her.
Madeleine Dad, I am not hard. I'd share anything with her . . . honest I would, only she's such a born grabber.
John (*with mock abhorrence*) Do you say so? Lock her up, why don't we? (*Pause*) Madeleine, her sort have had to go without since the year dot. Now, when her race is run, she sees the new lot having it soft. So she grabs. As you yourself said . . . the boldness of her! (*He puts down his cup*) I enjoyed that. Time I was on the move.
Tom Move . . . moving. I forgot. (*He goes out quickly into the garden*)
John What's up?
Tom (*to the Removals Man*) Sound man, you're still with us. I was afraid you'd gone home.
Removals Man Us? Not a fear of it. We're on double duty. We have to see the story out.
Tom Ah.
Removals Man Dowse the lights and turn the key in the door. So to speak.
Tom Yes, well, I'll settle up with you. (*He finds money and counts out the correct sum*)
John I'll say goodbye, so. Madeleine . . . Karl (*an amused inflexion on the name*). Enjoy your film. (*He goes into the garden*)

Tom is now having an altercation with the Removals Man, who is refusing the money offered

Madeleine God, but he gets up your nose. He can't look at an egg without telling you the agony the hen went through.
Karl He thinks they call him "Topsy Turvey" at school.

Madeleine gives a low-pitched machine-gun laugh

Well, they don't. You want to know? They call him "Scurvy Turvey."

Madeleine's laugh becomes louder and more staccato

Removals Man I'm not taking money for work that wasn't done.
John Tom, I'm off.
Tom Herself made a mistake. Now don't put us to shame. Help me out . . . come on.
Removals Man (*accepting the money*) Tell you what. I'll give a half-crown of it to the lad. And seeing as you have a great little garden at the back, I'll drop you in the few cabbage plants.
Tom Grand.
Removals Man One thing more. You'll have this. (*He offers Tom the bottle of stout that was intended for the Assistant*) Now yes, you will.
Tom (*accepting it, looking upward*) If she looks out, I'm knackered.
John Tom, I'm off. Say thanks to Ellie for me.
Tom I'll see you Monday. Kitchen table, nine o'clock.
John Sure. And the house is tremendous . . . you deserve it. And thanks for making me welcome.
Tom We thought you were someone else. Go home.
John (*seized by shyness*) No, I mean it. For Christ's sake, why should I, a man of as yet undiscovered genius, bother with an ignoramus so thick that in spite of the history of the world he'll swear on a stack of prayer-books that tomorrow will be great? I'll tell you why I bother with you. No one else will have me. (*He comes as close as he has ever done or ever will do to putting a hand on Tom's shoulder*)
Tom Listen, feck off.
John Yeah.

John nods to the Removals Man and goes off briskly

Tom takes the opened bottle

Removals Man A clever fellow, that . . . hard to keep up with.
Tom (*drinking*) I never try. G'luck.
Madeleine (*to Karl*) So what old picture are you going to?
Karl Dunno yet if I'll be let. The Astoria.
Madeleine Oh, that. You can save your one-and-ninepence. Cut to ribbons.
Karl (*in dismay*) It's not.

Madeleine Cis Cafferky saw it. She says, the minute your one goes to show a bit of leg there's a jump to something else.

Karl Ah, God . . . you can't read what you want, you can't see what you want. I'm fed up. And it's all so harmless.

Madeleine If it's all so . . . (*mimicking him, fondly*) . . . haaarmless, what has you so hot and bothered? You're a dirty little divil, aren't you?

Karl Dry up.

Madeleine So what's up with Dad? Why mightn't you be let go to the pictures?

Karl Dunno if I want to, now. I was in hopes, you see, that an inch of leg would turn me into a sex maniac.

Madeleine Now stop, I'll go red.

Karl We're in gaol here, do you know that? Jesus God, when I think of Scurvy Turvey dinning it into us that the *English* were tyrants.

Madeleine Answer me. I thought Dad 'ud be dug out of you. What for?

Karl Haven't a clue.

Pause

Madeleine Are you fond of him?

Karl (*alarmed*) What?

Madeleine Of him and Mam. Are you?

Karl What kind of question is that?

Madeleine What's wrong with it?

Karl Mad, what age are you? I mean, asking a fellow what he thinks of his parents . . . well, it's not . . . nice.

Madeleine Why isn't it? If you can't say it now, when can you say it?

Karl Never, full stop. Now grow up.

Madeleine I think Dad is great, so I do. I might even tell him.

Karl God, not while I'm listening. Mad, you have no shame.

Madeleine I think he's great because . . .

Karl walks away and sticks his fingers in his ears

I don't know why. Yes, I do . . . no, wait. Because . . . because in all his life my Dad never had a cygnet that wasn't a swan. There, now! Karl . . . I'm done. (*Loudly*) I say, I said it. Oh, yeah and another thing. He's . . .

Karl (*sticking his fingers back in his ears*) I'm not listening!

Ellie returns from upstairs and gives him a passing slap

Ellie Stop that shouting . . . from today out we have next-door neighbours. What are you at?

Karl Nothing.

Madeleine hisses at Karl, who has again taken his fingers from his ears

Madeleine He's a dote!

Karl Shurrup.

Madeleine Mam, Boland's Biscuits is opening a new factory in Dean's Grange.

Ellie (*knowing what is coming*) That so? Aren't they great!

Madeleine They're gumming for people to work for them. Can I take a job, Mam? For the summer. Can I?

Ellie No.

Madeleine Ah, Mam.

Ellie Holidays aren't for working in. You'll do as you're told and enjoy yourself.

Madeleine Everyone's earning money. Why can't I?

Ellie Because there's time enough. And don't put a face on you . . . you won't be let go short.

Madeleine (*almost in tears*) I want to pay my own way. It's so humiliating.

Ellie watches her for a moment

Ellie Yous are in such a mad tearing rush to be grown up. When it comes, yous'll soon get tired of it.

Karl (*gloomily*) Yeah, you wait till you're my age.

Ellie (*to business*) Madeleine. I've put the bedclothes back in your room, but I'm not going to make your bed for you as well. So do it now.

Madeleine Where's Granny?

Ellie In the sulks . . . where is she ever? And be a help . . . make Dympna's bed as well. There's a good girl.

Madeleine goes upstairs

Ellie Charlie, is your father gone out?

Karl In the garden.

Removals Man (*to Tom*) Watch it.

Tom splutters over his stout and thrusts the bottle at the Removals Man

Ellie goes to the front door

Ellie Excuse me. Tom can I see you?
Tom Sure. (*He returns to the house*)
Ellie What were you doing?
Tom Nothing.
Ellie Yes, you were. You were gosthering. Did you pay him the five shillings?
Tom Yes.
Ellie And not the seven-and-sixpence?
Tom (*lying*) No.
Ellie (*looking at him sceptically*) I have to give the kitchen a going over . . . there's grease on the draining board you could fry eggs in. Will you finish up what's in here?
Tom You carry on.
Ellie Charlie, you're to help him.

Ellie goes into the kitchen

Tom resumes unpacking one of the tea chests. Karl goes unenthusiastically to lend a hand

Karl Dad . . .
Tom So . . . are you off to see this "She's Doing Her . . ." whatever it is?
Karl No. Mad says it's all cut to bits, so I thought I might go to the Adelphi.
Tom What's on there?
Karl *Yield to the Night.* (*He has the blurb memorised*) It's a sensational film laying bare a woman's soul, and it is Diana Dors's first dramatic role.
Tom Sounds good, so.

They work for a moment, then Tom speaks, lowering his voice lest Ellie overhear from the kitchen

Why have you been missing Mass?
Karl What?
Tom Keep your voice down. And if you tell me it's none of my business, then I *will* give you a belt. Oh yeah, you're going on nineteen, a big fella. Well, I don't care if you're going on ninety, you've been off gallivanting instead of at Mass.
Karl Who says so?

Tom You were seen.

Karl Where?

Tom I'm asking you, is it true?

Karl It was Scurvy Turvey.

Tom Who?

Karl He thought we didn't see him slinking past with the dog. Then the rotten sod went and split on us.

Tom Never you mind your name-calling. I asked was it true?

Karl (*indignantly*) Well, honest to God. (*Then*) You said to be straight with you, so if you want to know, I think Mass is a load of old rubbish. And so is the rest of it.

Tom I see.

Karl I mean, God up there in the sky, spying on us. Dad, it's bilge.

Karl takes courage from Tom's silence

I mean, say you're a walking saint, and you commit the one bad sin in all your life . . . sixth commandment, like. So you do it, and before you can go to confession you're under the wheels of a bus. Do you know what God says? He says: "Ha, ha . . . gotcha!" (*He makes a thumbs-down sign*) I mean, give it a rest, what sort of thicks do they take us for?

Tom says nothing for a moment

I suppose there goes *Yield to the Night*.

Tom Why didn't you tell us?

Karl You know why. Mam would have had carnaptions.

Tom I wouldn't've.

Karl No?

Tom Do you see me having them?

Karl Look, I didn't want to . . .

Tom Keep it down.

Karl . . . to hurt your feelings.

Tom Then you made a right fist of it, didn't you?

Karl Sorry.

Tom Look, I don't give a toss what you believe in. What are you anyway, one of them atheists? Because, if you are, it's too soon. There ought to be an age for it, like taking a jar or driving a motor car.

Karl So what do *you* think.

Tom What about?

Karl About God. About going to Mass and stuff.

Tom I don't think about it. We're not supposed to think about it.

Karl That's great!

Tom Yes, it *is* great, because it's there for us and it always will be. Like a plate that's been set in front of us.

Karl A nice piece of cod.

Tom raises his hand

(*As before*) I said don't.

Tom Please.

Karl Please. (*Then*) No need to get huffy. All I'm asking is, do you and Mam go to Mass because you believe in it? Or do you go the way Granny and her lot do, because you're afraid not to?

Tom makes no answer

Which?

Tom One day, boy, you'll get sense. I'll talk to you then.

Karl (*in protest*) Dad!

Tom Son, go to Mass or don't go to Mass . . . what annoys me is the deception. Don't you know by now—and that applies to Madeleine and Colm and Dympna—you discuss anything with me . . . whatever's under the sun?

Karl Yeah?

Tom Certainly, yeah! In our house, time I was growing up, there was the ma and the da and me, and the three of us were as shy as mice, and the older I got the worse it was. Oh sure there'd be talk, yeah, about what won the three-thirty and how Sonny Doyle, Lord have mercy, was a sleeveen, and Kruger Kinsella was a hook. No, it wasn't talk, never talk, only oul' chat. It covered up what the silence wouldn't let be said. Maybe the old people thought bad of me because my life was still to live and theirs was done. So we made strange. And I decided, none of that in my house. Here there is no toss that cannot be argued. Have you me?

Karl Yes, Dad.

Tom We are not go-be-the-walls.

Karl No, Dad.

Tom Grand so. (*Exultant, meaning it*) Hey, do you know we're off to a great start? This must be the best day of my life. And so it is. (*He takes money from his pocket*) How much is the pictures?

Karl Pardon me? No, no, I'm . . .

Tom Yes, you will . . . seeing the day that's in it. And not a word to your mother about what we . . . ah . . . (*with a conspiratorial wink*) When it comes to religion she hasn't a lot of give in her.

During this, Ellie comes in

Ellie Who hasn't?

Tom (*without effort*) Herself upstairs.

Ellie Pity about her. The sink is as clean as it will ever be . . . Charlie, will you put away the bits of delph and stuff for me.

Karl You told me to . . .

Ellie I know what I told you. Now I'm telling you to the differ.

Karl I don't know what goes where.

Ellie Things'll go where they're put. Now stir yourself.

Karl goes into the kitchen

Ellie stays. Plainly she has something on her mind and it will take an effort on her part to give voice to it. Tom takes another object from the tea-chest

Tom This one's nearly empty . . . we're flying. Anything up?

Ellie It came to me when I was inside doing the shelves. In me life I never seen shelves the like of them. When you put a finger on them, it isn't wood at all, it's more like silk. You got Mr. Comerford to put them up for us, special. And all the thanks I gave you was dog's abuse. You must take me for a right b.

Tom (*mocking her*) Oh, a proper.

Ellie You doing the best you can for all of us . . . me spoiling it on you.

Tom You'd have your work cut out.

Ellie It's true what you said. I'm a coward . . . I know I am. I keep thinking, what if it goes wrong? If maybe one of the children gets sick? Or yourself?

Tom Me? Little fear of it.

Ellie (*with a flash of tartness*) Bless yourself when you say that! Or if an'thin' happened to Mr Cussens. If he maybe died and the shop 'ud have to be sold.

Tom Don't stop there. What if the sky fell in? Where the hell do you get the ideas from?

Ellie I don't know. When I think of paying out two thousand, three hundred pounds for a place to live in . . . honest, I have a cramp in the pit of my stomach.

Tom You're looking at it upside down. We've done what the old people could never do . . . we're going to live in our own house.

Ellie Tom, will you get sense? Four pounds to pay every week for twenty years . . . it's not the house that's being owned – it's us. There, you see? I'm doing it again.

Tom Ellie, if you don't take the first step, you'll never walk.

Ellie I know, I know.

Tom And you've no need to worry about Mr Cussens. That's taken care of.

Ellie You fixed it for him to live forever. I see.

Tom I was going to keep this as a surprise for you. I thought maybe it'd make a sort of Christmas box . . . put a bit of extra jizz in the day, like. Still, if it'll take a weight off your mind.

Ellie Then say it. (*A sense of foreboding makes her hand move involuntarily towards her abdomen, but the urge is resisted*)

Tom Mr C. is pushing the seventy mark, and the shop's getting too much for him. He says I'm to have first refusal.

Ellie How? Of what?

Tom To buy the shop. Isn't it great?

Ellie (*faintly*) Oh, my God. (*Her hand now clutches her abdomen as if she has been seized by a cramp. She sits*)

Tom Another two years and I'll be my own boss. So how's that for news?

Ellie At least you didn't keep it for Christmas.

Tom (*laughing*) If you could see yourself.

Ellie I'm weak with fright.

Tom Don't be. I have it worked out . . . it's a snip.

Ellie And I thought buying this place was bad enough.

Tom Look, trust me.

Ellie I do, I do, but it's no use, Tom, I'm hopeless. I'm not the right kind of wife for you.

Tom It's too late to change now. We can't give the kids back.

Ellie I mean it. You ought to have married someone like Colleen.

This comes as a sudden blow, although perhaps not intended as such. It is a few moments before Tom feels the impact

She'd be in her element. Give her a dare, and whatever it was she'd do it. She'd have newness if it killed her.

Tom What sort of a thing was that to say?

Ellie What?

Tom That I ought to have . . . (*He cannot complete the sentence*) . . . About your sister.

Ellie Her name was Colleen.

Tom About Colleen.

He is angry and a little scared. She has for the first time crossed the threshold of a private world and has said what he himself has never acknowledged

Ellie It's true. Moving into a new house . . . God, she'd have loved that.

Tom Peculiar sort of remark to make.

Ellie Why is it? (*Whatever emotional stresses lie under the surface, Ellie's voice is calm, her manner matter-of-fact*)

Tom Her and me . . . that's the best ever.

Ellie Do you remember the White Cottage? On Killiney Strand?

Tom No.

Ellie (*with quiet certainty*) Yes, you do. The Sunday evening I was there with Colleen. I remember every bit of it. How Mibs Tate went up on the railway bank with Lar Kearns, and she married him, and that was the end of her and Dessie Drumm, who was wild out about her. And Colleen had on a cornflower blue dress with a white collar. You came over. You asked her to dance, and she said no, 'cause the doctor had told her she wasn't to. So you went up to the leader of the band, the cheek of you, and, even though it was a ceilidhr and old-time, they played a slow waltz for the pair of you. Except that in the wind-up Colleen still wouldn't dance with you. So I did.

Tom You have a good memory.

Ellie For that night, I do. We had to go home early on account of Colleen, and you walked us up the path to the station. I remember, like it was now, the sound of the waves in the dark when I went off down the platform so as you could ask her to go out with you.

Tom If I did, she said no.

Ellie She was sick. She wanted to have a bit of gas. You'd have moped around after her, wanting her to be serious, no one else in the world but the pair of yous.

Tom Yes, well, she's not in it any longer, so we'll have done.

Ellie I do often wonder if you talk to her.

Tom If I do what?

Ellie I get queer ideas. I think: maybe now she goes out with him, dead and all as she is. I'd be jealous of that. I'd mind it if I thought

you showed her this house . . . the rooms in it and the bit of garden
at the back. Maybe you told her about buying the shop off Mr
Cussens. Did you? I suppose she said: "Good man, yourself, more
power to you. Don't mind Ellie . . . all she's good for is taking the
good out of it." Did she say that to you?

He looks at her with great sadness

What's up, Tom? Is she not there anymore? Did I hunt her on you?
If so, you have no call to be vexed. I was tired all these years of
acting the goosegob with the pair of you. (*She gives his arm a small
affectionate squeeze; it is probably as demonstrative as she can get*)
Hey . . . now what's the long face for? You have the house, and
before long there'll be the shop as well. And in the heel of the hunt,
isn't it like you said . . . they won't take the children back.

The Removals Man comes to the door

Removals Man Mr N . . . are you there?
Tom (*going to him*) Hello.
Removals Man Half-time whistle, Mr N., the hour is gone and the
story's told. Time Eamonn and me was knocking off.
Tom You were great. Thanks very much.
Removals Man What great? . . . we'll see you next time.
Tom Will I just . . . shut up shop then?
Removals Man The same as you do at Cussens's? Why don't you.

*They shake hands. The Removals Man and Eamonn watch as Tom
enters the house*

*Madeleine comes downstairs, again in her fantasy film world, her face
uplifted, radiant*

*What follows is still realistic, but slightly idealized, as befits Tom's
wishful vision of family*

Removals Man (*to us*) There's Audrey again. When you're a princess and
duty calls, true love is always down the field. It's a hard old station.
Ellie Madeleine, you'll trip over something. A charity if you weren't
left that way.
Madeleine (*abdicating*) I did my bed and Dympna's, like you said.
Mam, can I go over to Monica Mulhall's? She's going to lend me
her Slim Whitman singing *Rose Marie*, and I'm going to teach her
the Yo-Yo.

Tom The yo-yo? Is that thing back again?

Madeleine Dad, it's a dance. (*She demonstrates, providing her own vocal music*)

Through this Karl comes downstairs

Ellie Will you stop . . . you'd give a body's eyes a headache.

Karl Mam, I'm going over to the old house.

Ellie To Creebrishta? What for?

Karl For the cat. He doesn't know we moved.

Ellie Oh, poor old Mog, neither does he. He'll be crying in the empty house. Yes, son, go and get him. Run.

The Removals Man coughs gently; a reminder to Tom

Tom (*to the Removals Man*) I'm trying to get a word in. Ellie . . . kids, the man says we're to finish up.

Ellie Cheek of him. I have the tea to get.

Madeleine And I promised Monica.

Tom Yes . . .

Karl And there's Mog, on his ownsome.

Tom (*distracted*) Mog, Monica, Monica, Mog. Another half-minute won't . . .

Ellie Wait. (*She has seen the wrapped picture*) What's this? Is it ours?

Tom Where? No, it's John's. He came in with it. (*He detaches the envelope attached to the wrapping paper*) It's for us. "To Ellie and Tom".

Ellie Oh, he didn't. Would you be up to him?

Tom unwraps it. It is a large, framed print of an Irish landscape, possibly a Paul Henry. There is a thatched cottage to the fore

Tom Hey, how about this, then?

Ellie Oh, it's gorgeous, he oughtn't've. It's down the country, isn't it? Charlie . . . ah, look.

Karl Yeah, terrific. Dad, I have to go.

Ellie Is there a card with it? What's it say?

Tom Give us a chance. "Lest . . . lest we forget." Good old John.

Ellie He's a dote.

Karl Dad, I am half-way up the road.

Madeleine We both are. Will you hurry up.

Tom Now yous have me flustered. (*To Ellie*) God, in our young day, if we'd had the chances this pair have now, we'd have conquered the world.

Ellie Say what you have to say.

Tom I'm trying to.

Ellie And don't go dipping your bread in it.

Tom Right. (*With a small clearing of the throat*) John, who gave us this, and the old woman upstairs, the pair of them belongs to what's past and done with. He wants to; she has to. But not us, no one in this room. The here-and-now is what's ours, and whatever's in front of us will be good because we'll make it good.

Removals Man And God bless his innocence.

Tom (*dismissing them*) That's it. All done. (*He sits on the sofa*)

In response, Ellie, Madeleine and Karl disperse—not so much in character as actors quitting a stage. There is a far-off thunderclap and the soft sound of rain

Removals Man Down it comes, Eamonn, on the dot. Come on, boy, run for the van.

The Removals Man and his Assistant run off

Colleen comes and sits on the arm of the sofa next to Tom. She wears a cornflower blue dress with a white collar. She is eighteen; for her the year is nineteen-thirty-five. Her cheeks have the hectic flush of the consumptive

Tom Because . . . because time is not the boss. We are.

CURTAIN

PART TWO

It is Saturday, July 11th, 1987

As the CURTAIN *rises a few major pieces of furniture are already in place. These are of good quality and tasteful; this is not the home of wealthy people, but the carpet, the armchairs, the coffee table and the occasional pieces tell us that the Noones are either comfortably off or have made an act of faith in their furniture. There are two tea-chests, as in Part One; also, there is again a pile of household effects covered by a dust-sheet*

The beginning of Part One is repeated. As the Lights begin to come up, the Removals Man and his Assistant enter carrying a sofa between them—a good-quality, deep sofa. The Removals Man directs that it should be placed facing front. When it is in position, they remove the dust cover, revealing a TV set on a purpose-made trolley, with a VCR underneath, music centre, a couple of expensive table lamps and an occasional table or small bureau. The Assistant disposes of the lamps and music centre while the Removals Man moves the TV and VCR to a position down-stage right and plugs them in. By now, the House Lights have gone down. The Removals Man is dressed as before: the Assistant wears jeans now

Removals Man (*with a flourish*) Now!

And once again the house is erected. As before, it is not so much shown as suggested, but the shape is less conventionally boxlike; being detached, it is not a rubber-stamp version of its next-door neighbour. This, then, is Number 14, Martello Lawn. A car door is heard slamming. The Removals Man looks off anxiously.

Front door, if you please . . . thank you!

The front door is flown into position. The Removals Man is just in time to open it

Ellie enters. She is thirty-nine, as before, but now she looks younger and is dressed simply, yet with style. Since it is summer, she perhaps wears a quilted, sleeveless jacket over a well-cut shirt. In each hand she carries silver-foil supermarket bags, fully laden and bearing the name "Tru-Valu".

Removals Man Mrs Noone, ma'am . . . if I may be so forward . . .
Ellie Oh, there you are . . . hello.
Removals Man . . . as to bid you a hearty welcome to the new . . .
Ellie Thanks. Sorry . . . talk about a lazy man's load. (*To herself*) Kitchen . . . kitchen.
Removals Man Can I give you a . . . (*He is too late*)

Ellie crosses and goes out quickly, hurrying to set the bags down before they can slip and fall

The Removals Man is slightly taken aback

Assistant Took the wind out of your sails.
Removals Man What? Not at all. We'll make a start on the tea-chests.
Assistant Sorry . . . I'm jacking it.
Removals Man Ah, now wait.
Assistant No way.
Removals Man (*an appeal*) Eamonn . . .
Assistant Look, I could have sloped off, couldn't I, like Ger and Shamy? But no, softy here put in two extra hours. That's it . . . finito.
Removals Man Eamonn, it's the weekend. We can't see them stuck.
Assistant (*launching into jargon*) Mr M., pending further talks with management, three o'clock of a Saturday continues to be deemed unsocial hours, and my neck's out far enough.
Removals Man (*mildly*) You do know I'm the gaffer on this job.
Assistant Get away.
Removals Man So I've been led to believe.
Assistant Martin, we're not in old God's time. No one orders no one any more.
Removals Man (*changing his tack*) The story has to be told.
Assistant Tell it. Where's your hindrance?
Removals Man (*a last appeal*) Will we at least tidy up for them?
Assistant (*indicating the audience*) They're waiting.

The Removals Man sighs and acknowledges our existence

Removals Man It's the eleventh of July, nineteen-eighty-seven, a Saturday, and this is Number Fourteen, Martello Lawn. (*He considers the word*) Lawn . . . it has a nice greeny well-off sound to it. A bit grander than the rest of them, the Avenues and Crescents, and the Closes and Groves? It's more of a one with the Oakses and Beeches, the Meadowses and Paddocks?

Assistant Tell us, whatever happened to saints' names?

Removals Man Whatever happened to saints? Today the Noones are moving here from Creebrishta Park . . . on the site of where the nurseries used to be, and the old house before them. A nice place, the Park, much aspired to, but the Lawn is a step up. You could say that the grass is greener.

Ellie returns

Ellie I'm sorry. I daren't stop . . . eggs and stuff. You were saying?

Removals Man Yes. Ah . . . Eamonn . . .

Assistant (*abdicating*) You tell it . . . you're the gaffer.

Removals Man The . . . ah, way it is, ma'am, as of yesterday, there's been what you might call an industrial grey area.

Ellie (*at once*) You're on strike.

Removals Man What? A strike? Eamonn, do you hear her? Not at all. All there is is a sort of a class of a go-slow. We'll be back on the job nine sharp on Monday. Nine for a quarter past, says you.

Ellie You're not going off home on us? You can't. Have you seen in there . . . in my kitchen?

Removals Man I know, sure I know.

Ellie And you're saying we're to be left for the weekend? No, it's a joke. Is it a joke?

Removals Man Terrible.

There is a mumbled, echoing "Terrible" from the Assistant

Ellie It's a disgrace. My husband is paying you overtime.

Removals Man Now there you've no worries. None. The company'll make full adjustment. Yous'll not be let down.

Ellie Won't we? A go-slow, is that what you said? Over what?

Assistant Gloves.

Ellie Excuse me?

Assistant Work gloves. We can't hump packing cases with our bare hands, can we?

Removals Man The lady only asked a question.

Assistant I'm telling her. (*To Ellie*) Management sees fit to reject our claim for replacement gloves. Sign's on it, we're refusing to wear out the ones we have.

Ellie Gloves.

Assistant Uh-huh.

Ellie And we have no beds to sleep in.

Removals Man Yes, you do. Eamonn, go upstairs . . .

Assistant Hey, hey, hey . . .

Removals Man We're not savages, put the beds up for them. Sound man, you'll do it flying. Your good deed for the day.

The Assistant levels a forefinger at him, moving it slowly up and down, as if keeping his temper. It is an admission of impotence. He goes towards the stairs

The Assistant exits upstairs

Ellie Thanks.

Removals Man He has a soft heart, he ought to be in the scouts. Inside, now . . . how are you for cooking? Have we lift-off?

Ellie We'll manage. Somehow.

Removals Man What's a day-and-a-bit of roughing it? And you have a beautiful house, ma'am . . . may you never fall out in it or with it.

Ellie (*suitably modest*) It's a bit roomier than we're used to.

Removals Man Will you go 'way. Yous'll wear it like a skin.

She smiles, accepting the compliment

Still, you don't feel at all nervous?

Ellie How?

Removals Man It's an important step. There's many a person I move and she says to me: "Are we not maybe taking on too much?" Or "Sure weren't we grand the way we were?"

She looks at him. She is not offended, but in this second part of the play there exists a greater distance between Ellie and the Removals Man. Unlike the former Ellie, she is not glad of the familiarity. As for the Removals Man, he has endeavoured to pull the story back on its former tracks

It's true as I'm standing.

Ellie People say that to you?

Removals Man The odd one.
Ellie They must be. (*It is a small rebuff*)
Removals Man Yes, well . . . I ought to stop putting in me prate.

For Ellie, the greater evil would be if she appeared stand-offish. She over-compensates

Ellie You didn't. No such thing.
Removals Man Too much old talk . . .
Ellie Don't be silly.
Removals Man Still and all, I . . .
Ellie (*overlapping*) The first time we . . .

He stands back, as it were, allowing her to go first

Ellie Nothing. I mean, the day Tom . . . the day my husband sailed in and landed us with what was as good as a . . . well, it's what they call a *fait accompli* . . .

The Removals Man nods gravely

I said: "What? Us, move out of Creebrishta? You're mad." And of course the bold Tom trotted out figures and sums, and his company had this scheme I couldn't make head nor tail of, begging us to borrow off them, and in the end I said to him: "Do it then, but let it be a house where for once I haven't to listen to the next-door neighbour stirring his tea." So in the wind-up here we are. (*She gives a small, self-conscious laugh*)
Removals Man This is the house for you, so. You could shoot a person, and no one 'ud hear. (*Straight-faced*) I mean, God forbid.
Ellie Indeed.
Removals Man Ma'am, excuse me. The lad upstairs isn't to know where the beds go. If you had a word with him, it'd stand to you.
Ellie I never thought. And thanks . . . thanks for . . .
Removals Man Go on.

Ellie goes towards the stairs and moves out of sight

The Removals Man watches her

Time nudging and shoving them; them prodding time and nudging it. And time making a hames of our story on us.

Tom Noone appears in the garden area. He wears a business suit. He looks at the house; his manner is more restrained than in nineteen-fifty-seven

There he is now. T.J. Noone. Tom. Forty-two, going on . . . forty-three. He's the manager of Tru-Valu out beyant at what they call The Mall. Branch manager, that is. A decent skin, they'll tell you, them that's under him. Being liked doesn't put money in a till, but Tom makes up for his handicap by working that bit extra. He met herself, Ellie Quirke-that-was, beyant in London.

Tom At a social.

Removals Man Nineteen-sixty-six. He was doing a training course; she was on a holiday. With her sister, Coll—

Tom Ingrid.

Removals Man Her sister Ingrid. Her mother named her after a one that used to be in the films.

Tom Ingrid Bergman, that is. Dead now.

Removals Man He means the film star is. Herself's sister isn't. She's a reflection of the nation's improving health. Couldn't be fitter.

Ellie (*from upstairs*) T.J., are you home?

Tom I took two hours off.

Ellie Well, there's news, and you won't like it.

Tom What?

Ellie Ask the man. And don't stand gawking at the house. People will think we won it.

Removals Man T.J. and Ellie were married in 'sixty-nine. Two children, eighteen and seventeen. There's a cat, too; it's up the town. (*He goes to the door to greet Tom*) Afternoon, Mr N. Big day for you.

Tom My wife tells me there's news I'm not going to like.

Removals Man Oh, that must be about the withdrawal of labour.

Tom Labour? Do you mean yours?

Removals Man A passing cloud, sir.

Tom For God's sake . . .

Removals Man Sunshine on Monday, guaranteed.

Tom *Monday*?

Removals Man Further outlook: set fair.

Tom Jesus. Look is this in any way our fault?

Removals Man (*beaming*) Yours? Not at all. The . . .

Tom Good. Because I wouldn't like to think that my wife had maybe stinted on the tea-bags when she was brewing up for your lot.

Removals Man Very good. Excellent.

Tom (*with a flare-up of anger*) No, I mean it . . . but bugger it!

Removals Man Right!

Tom Well, if you can't cure it, endure it. Fact of life.

He walks into the house, nodding, considering. In the case of whatever has to do with the external world, he is a realist; we can almost see him coming to terms

(*Decisively*) We'll live.
Removals Man Grand.

The subject has been tucked away, and Tom is once again in good humour

Tom There was a time when Mrs Noone . . . there was a time when Ellie and I thought that even Creebrishta Park 'ud be out of our class. It was for the nobs and the young execs. We saw the bulldozers take away the nurseries and the old gate lodge, and we saw the new estate go up. And we said, the hell with it, we'll chance our arm with the rest of them. So I put down the deposit with my breath in my fist—true!—and we moved in, and weren't we great? . . . we . . . lived in Creebrishta! And now we're reneging on it for this.
Removals Man Reneging? Not at all. You're making room for the next man.
Tom (*a pleasant realization*) So I am.
Removals Man Keep on the move, that's how it's done.
Tom Tell you what's great. What with the traffic, the town's a bottleneck. But as of today we're at the other end of it. So I save minutes getting to the job. (*His joke*) Have myself a lie-in!
Removals Man Trouble is, if you wanted to go the other way . . . out into Wicklow . . .
Tom Ah, well.
Removals Man . . . to Glendalough, maybe . . .
Tom Where's that then? No, at weekends the kids want to do their own thing. And I don't mind watching the box . . . a window on the world.

Ellie comes downstairs

The Removals Man takes out a packet of cigarettes

Removals Man Here's your good lady.
Tom So no problem.
Removals Man (*to Ellie*) Is he doing the needful?

Ellie (*not over-enthusiastic*) He's very obliging. Tom . . .
Removals Man Ma'am, excuse me. Do you mind if I light up?
Ellie What? Oh, you never do.
Tom We're off.
Ellie And at your age.
Removals Man Well . . . the odd time.
Ellie The odd time! Tom, will you look at his poor fingers. Oh, you
    silly man, do you not realize what the inside of your . . .
Tom *Ellie.*
Ellie What? (*Then, to the Removals Man*) I have a slate loose, don't
    mind me.
Tom It's her hobbyhorse. Light up, for God's sake.
Ellie Yes, do . . . do. Smoke!
Removals Man No, the woman is right, it's disgusting. I think I'll wait
    in the garden for the young lad. Bit of fresh air. (*He goes out to the
    garden*)
Tom Look, will you stay and . . . (*He breaks off*)

*In the wake of the Removals Man, Ellie fans away non-existent cigarette
smoke. In the garden, the Removals Man lights up and takes a deep,
contented drag*

Ellie Well, did you hear the mess we're in?
Tom Yeah, I got the full weather report.
Ellie The what?
Tom "Further outlook: fair." The jargon people come out with!
Ellie We've been left high and dry.
Tom (*employing his own jargon*) Yes, I've taken all that on board.
Ellie (*pointing upstairs*) And that little bastard was rude to me. I'm raging.
Tom (*his jargon again*) I hear what you say.
Ellie Well, then . . . what?
Tom You don't know me yet, do you?

He makes to put his arms around her. She resists

Ellie Stop messing and tell me.
Tom Try this for size. At six o'clock—three hours' time—the staff at
    Tru-Valu will clock out. Quarter *past* six, on your doorstep there'll
    be four dirty great Goliaths out of our stock-room . . .
Ellie Tom, you're brilliant.
Tom We'll get our pair to put in their tuppence worth, and by eight
    o'clock . . .

Ellie Fantastic. But it's Saturday night . . . maybe your lot will want to go to the pub or a disco or . . .

Tom I do them favours . . . they'll be glad to get out from under. Anyway, on what Tru-Valu pays them they can't afford discos.

Ellie You brat, you.

Tom So what do you say to me now?

Ellie You're . . . not . . . bad.

He moves to hug her again. She offers her cheek and pushes him away with a small groan as if she were too easily aroused

Christ.

She moves past him. The small rejection, if it is one, has been disguised as a compliment

Tom, do you know what he asked me? (*Pointing*) Him. Did I feel at all nervous?

Tom You? About what?

Ellie About this, the move. I thought, why would I be nervous?

Tom He was being chatty.

Ellie And now I *am* nervous.

Removals Man (*to us*) Thanks be to God. It's not an easy job telling the same tale twice. A few more quid in the bank, two less kids to break your heart over, four wheels under you. I hold out the same hoop for them and damned if the buggers'll jump.

Ellie Stop me from worrying. Explain it again.

Tom (*patiently, humouring*) The company has a plan. They give their top management a low-interest loan. It's their way of holding on to us but I'm happy where I am, so the joke's on them. See?

Ellie What if there's a catch to it?

The Removals Man laughs softly

Tom There isn't.

Ellie What if they go broke?

Tom They won't.

Ellie . . . "We've gone bust . . . where's what we lent you? . . . cough up."

Removals Man Yes, you can take the girl out of Creebrishta . . .

Tom Ellie, have sense, that's a thousand to one chance.

Ellie (*appalled*) Is that all?

Removals Man . . . but damned if you can take Creebrishta out of . . .

The Assistant comes downstairs noisily

Assistant I done it.
Ellie Thank you. (*To Tom*) He was putting up the beds for us.
Tom Blessings on you. There's a drop of beer inside in the fridge. Will you help yourself?
Assistant Ta.

The Assistant goes into the kitchen

Ellie Are you mad? That surly pup left us high and dry, he didn't even want to do the beds, only he was made, and you tell him to help himself.
Tom Yes, because never give that type an excuse to be bolshie.
Ellie Your head is gone, you know that? He doesn't *need* an excuse. He . . . (*She breaks off*)

The Assistant returns. He is carrying an entire six-pack of lager

Ellie and Tom stare at him

Assistant Guh luck. (*He crosses without pausing and goes into the garden*)
Ellie I've been struck blind. I don't believe it. Get our beer back.
Tom You get it back.

The Assistant tosses a can to the Removals Man

Removals Man Good man. (*Sticking his head in*) Thanks very much.
Tom (*warmly*) You're welcome.
Ellie (*ditto; overlapping*) Not at all!
Removals Man And I think you're having visitors. A couple of ladies.
Ellie Mammy said she'd drop in. Maybe she brought Ingrid?
Tom Maybe Sodom would be seen without Gomorrah.
Ellie Now be polite. Help me tidy up here. Poor Ingrid.

Tom shrugs

You've such a down on her.

During the next scene, before Mary and Ingrid enter the house, Ellie goes to the kitchen and returns with a tray of mixed drinking glasses and Tom unwraps potted plants

By now the Removals Man and the Assistant are sunning themselves and enjoying their beers. The Assistant has opened his shirt to the waist

Mary Quirke and her daughter Ingrid appear. Mary is sixty-four, but in her appearance she could be five years younger. She enjoys her creature comforts; unlike her nineteen-fifty-seven version, she is not haunted by the bitterness of knowing that the remainder of her life will be downhill. She is better spoken than the Mary of nineteen-fifty-seven. Ingrid is two years older then Ellie and looks it. Once attractive, she has become overblown and is now lumpish, in figure and in personality. She is fascinated by the house

Removals Man 'Afternoon, ladies. The day kept up.
Mary Ah, what happened? Did your deck chair collapse on you?
Removals Man Eamonn, say nothing.
Assistant Abou' wha?
Removals Man Don't waste your lightning repartee on her. She's too sharp. (*To Mary*) So what do you think?
Mary It's nice. It's very nice, yes, it is. It wouldn't be my style, mind. Would it be your style, Ingrid?

Ingrid, in her own world, stares at the house

I could never be ostentatious. I haven't the head for it.

When Ingrid speaks it is in a calm affirmative manner, as if it were only by a fluke of nature that the new house is Ellie's and not hers

Ingrid I wouldn't have gravel there . . . it only makes work, I'd have crazy paving. And you can see part of the tank for the heating. I'd put up a trellis to hide it. Anyway, I wouldn't have oil; I'd have gas.
Mary Picking and choosing. There was a time it was so cold I put yourself and Ellie to bed early because it saved lighting a fire. Would you credit that?
Ingrid Number fourteen. No, I'd have a name on the front. "San Pedro", maybe, after our holiday. Or "Edelweiss" or "Song of the Sea".
Removals Man Excuse me, ladies . . .
Ingrid I'd have a bathroom suite, all in . . .
Mary Ingrid, the man's talking.
Removals Man Thank you.
Ingrid . . . in lemon.

Removals Man Mrs Quirke lives with her older girl, Ingrid, in one of the quarry cottages. The people there no longer eat their young; nowadays instead, they paint their front doors red and daffodil . . .
Ingrid Ours is mauve.
Removals Man . . . and mauve. And cottages that once were small, are "bijou" now.
Mary It means with a bathroom.
Removals Man Ingrid works in the hot bread shop in the town, and Mrs Quirke has her widow's compensation. Her husband, Jimmy, put up aerials for Hillside Electric. He died . . . how long ago, Eamonn?
Assistant (*consulting his notebook*) November, nineteen sixty-three. Of an inter . . . (*the word defeats him*)
Removals Man Intercranial haemorrhage.
Mary Forty-four. It's too young.
Removals Man He took a fall at work. Not too bad of a fall, but good luck and Jim were never great. In 'sixty-three the medical vogue was all for concussion, so they treated him for that.
Mary It was in the papers. Everyone knew our business.
Removals Man Afterwards, you could have gone to live with your other girl and himself. Today, you could have been moving in here.
Mary What for? I told them no, it would cramp my style. No, I stayed with Ingrid.
Ingrid I could have got married. Wouldn't be bothered.
Mary Friday evenings, we take a drink. We go on all the outings and to whatever's on. I turn around and the week is gone on me. Ingrid is on the shop-fronts committee. We never stop.
Ingrid I could have married *him*. (*She nods towards the house*)
Mary Ingrid, no naming names.
Ingrid I could have.
Mary (*with an indulgent smile*) Shush up, you're bold. (*To the Removals Man*) So will we go in?

The Removals Man makes a gesture inviting her to do so

Come on, Ingrid.

The two enter the house

Mary Here's trouble-the-house. Ah, but you're up to your ears.
Ellie Not at all. Hello, Ingrid.
Mary Five minutes, then we're off.

Ingrid How are you, Tommy?
Ellie Answer.
Tom Terrific.

To an outsider, Ingrid's teasing manner towards Tom is so inoffensive as to make his response seem boorish. In reality, she is needling him; he has refused to defer to her private self-image, and beneath her manner there is a shrill unforgiveness

Mary Isn't it glorious weather?
Ellie Yes.
Mary I mean, for July.
Ellie Mammy, will you sit.
Mary No, no, I want to look.
Ingrid I'll plonk myself beside Tommy. I know he's too shy to ask.

Ingrid sits beside him, perhaps on an arm of the sofa, and makes as if to rumple his hair. He slants his head away from her hand. Ellie frowns at him as if to tell him to be sociable. It is no more than the smallest of moments

Mary (*looking about her*) It's peculiar how when the weather is bad it's brighter out.
Ellie Excuse me?
Mary I mean, how nowadays you never see a black umbrella. All the colours 'ud blind you. (*Giving her verdict on the house*) Yes, it's very nice, yes, it is.
Ellie (*coolly*) Thanks, Mammy, I'm glad you're so thrilled. Tom, will you go and get the . . . (*she indicates the glasses*).
Tom We were going to wait for the kids.
Ellie (*with a dig at Mary*) You heard what Mammy said. Herself and Ingrid are off in five minutes.
Tom Well, John said he'd come by and say hallo.
Ellie (*not pleased*) Did he?
Ingrid (*shrilly*) Who . . . John Turvey? *Him?*
Tom Yes, him.
Ingrid Huh. (*Giggling*) At least *I'*ll be safe.
Tom Damn sure you will. When weren't you?
Ellie Tom!
Tom No, I mean that's the kind of cheap, go-by-the-wall remark that's . . .

Ellie Will you do as I asked you? (*Then*) And if he's coming here you should have said.

Tom (*angrily*) *Why?*

She glares back, facing him. The moment holds, then:

Tom exits to the kitchen

Ingrid He's very prickly. Of course I know why.

Ellie He has a right to be. John Turvey and he are . . .

Ingrid Conscience.

Ellie What?

Ingrid Because he has me on his conscience.

Ellie Oh, for God's sake.

Ingrid (*with calm certainty*) I know him of an old date. That's why he can't bear to be touched or talked to. Whenever I try to have a . . . a . . . a bit of gas with him, he snaps like an old dog a sign on a gate'd say beware of.

Ellie One day they're going to lock you up.

Ingrid You're as bad.

Ellie How, am I?

Ingrid For taking his part.

Ellie Ingrid . . .

Ingrid See? She can't answer.

Ellie Ingrid, the kind of day today is for me, if it'd burn I'd put a match to it. So if you please, will you as long as you're here behave yourself.

Mary Mm . . . as long as she's here.

Ellie Excuse me?

Mary She's to mind her p's and q's. Oh, it's an old saying and a true one . . . put a beggar on horseback.

Ellie Us, do you mean? Tom and me?

Mary "Mammy and Ingrid have to be off in five minutes."

Ellie It's what you yourself said.

Mary It is, yes. And how quick you took me up on it.

During the following, Tom returns. He is carrying a bottle of champagne. He waits by the kitchen until Ellie has finished speaking

Ellie (*levelly*) Mammy, you waltzed in here and you looked at my house as if there was a bad smell in it.

Mary opens her mouth to speak

Yes, you did, so. "Mm, it's very nice, yes, it is." You're an old begrudger, and I gave you tit for tat. Well, I'm sorry, and stay as long as you like. And, Ingrid, you shut up.

Tom Hear, hear.

Ingrid Mammy, look, it's champagne.

Mary There's style.

Ellie We have it every afternoon.

Ingrid Tommy, Tommy, make it go pop.

Dismissively, Tom puts a finger in his cheek and makes a popping noise. The champagne, we see, is already opened

(*Disappointed*) Oh, he opened it.

Mary Don't be so childish.

Tom (*pouring*) Can't let the occasion go unmarked.

Ellie We haven't unpacked the right glasses . . . they're all mixed.

Mary Cups 'ud do us. Far from it we were reared.

Tom (*handing Mary a glass*) Here you go. Well, since we're in the house, we may as well live up to it. (*To Ingrid*) Yourself . . .

Ingrid Ellie, that wall. Do you know, I'm not mad keen on the colour.

Ellie (*agreeably*) Aren't you blest then, Ingrid, that you don't have to live with it?

Mary Still, you're the devils for style, yes, you are.

Tom Last night, too tired to sleep, I was thinking about our Madeleine. Don't know what put it into my head, but I thought won't this be a great house for her to get married out of.

Ellie You what?

Tom One day.

Ellie Do you hear him? He has the banns called and poor child not even going out with boys yet.

Tom She will, any day now.

Ellie I don't know. Whatever the new fad is, she's into it. Like me with the aerobics and the water-colouring. I spend so much time improving the quality of life that I have no life left to improve.

Mary Madeleine won't be left behind the door, no, she will not. Not like some.

Ingrid Not like me.

Mary Still Ingrid was fierce. A shocker.

Ingrid (*happily*) I was. God forgive me.

Mary It was my own fault. I blame myself, the name I gave her.

Ingrid Tell it, tell it.
Mary They have the story off by heart.
Ellie No, we don't.

As Tom seems about to speak, Ellie warns him with a look

Mary You're sick and tired of it. No . . . not if you paid me.
Tom Yes . . . well, listen. Here's to the house.
Mary And God send the pair of you good luck in it, yes, He will.

They drink. Ingrid does so greedily. Some champagne ascends into her nose. She splutters noisily and reaches in her bag for a tissue. The others ignore her

Ellie Mm . . . I could get used to this.
Tom Not bad.
Mary It's nice and cool. (*Straight into her tale*) Anyway, I christened her Ingrid after Ingrid Bergman. She was so wholesome, yes, she was. Ellie, did you ever see *The Bells of St. Mary's*, when she was the nun?

Ellie and Tom look at Ingrid who is making heavy weather of her repairs

And still and all, Father Kearney gave out yards to me. Were there not, he said, enough saints in the calendar without calling an unfortunate child Ingrid?
Ellie Tom . . . (*She indicates that he should refill Ingrid's glass*)
Mary Well, I wouldn't budge. I had my own way. Because this one was gorgeous, yes, you were. You'd look at her and you'd say, that could be Ingrid Bergman in her pram.

Ingrid gives her nose a final rub and picks up her glass

And how old were you? . . . only four or five, when didn't your one, the other one, leave her husband and run off to Italy with an Eyetie. Rosetti or someone. And Father Kearney came up to me in the town. "Are you satisfied now?" he said. "Oh, the child has a great future in front of her!" Lord have mercy on him, he was right. She was man-mad . . . oh, a breaker of hearts.
Ingrid I was.
Tom Still, she's passed her sell-by-date now.
Ellie Tom!
Ingrid What does that mean?
Ellie It's a joke. Don't mind him.

Ingrid looks at Tom for a moment

Ingrid Many's the time I'd see a nice boy in the town or at a hop and I'd say "Oh, he's the answer to my dreams." Only when I met him he'd maybe be rough or common . . . not nice at all. So that was that, only it was my mistake for thinking he was what he wasn't. I didn't blame him for it.

A moment's silence. Ingrid tastes her champagne

Champagne now is romantic.

John Turvey appears in the garden area with Carlos. As before, John is carrying a wrapped object that is obviously a wall picture. His age is unchanged from Part One. Probably he wears jeans. Carlos is 18

John (*to the Removals Man*) That's not too bad of a day. (*Calling into the house*) Is there anyone in residence?
Removals Man Great the way it held up for them.
Tom It's John. (*Calling*) Too late. We drank your drink.

The Assistant looks at John and sniggers

Assistant (*to the Removals Man*) Ehh . . . ehh . . .
Removals Man You dry up. (*To John*) Excuse me. (*To us*) Up until May, Mr Turvey was a teacher at St. Begnet's out on the new estate. Him and Tom Noone have been comrades since the year dot. You're glad of a friend the day the world won't wag with you. And this young fellow will be starting university in the autumn. Learning how to destroy the country, am I right?
Carlos (*taking the joke*) Yes . . . architecture.
Removals Man He's the Noones' only lad. Never a day's worry to either of them. Name of . . .
Carlos Carlos.
Removals Man Carlos.
John Not from affectation . . . more a mark of solidarity with . . . Nicaragua, is it?
Carlos Or Chile. Either one.

They go into the house. During the following, John will set down his picture as and where he did so in Part One. Carlos's attitude to John is friendlier than Karl's was in nineteen-fifty-seven, just as Ellie's, while amicable, is guarded and a little distant

John Hello.

Tom Would you be up to him, he heard the fizz. (*Proffering a glass*) Here, take hold of this.

John Hello, Ellie. Afternoon, Mrs Quirke . . . Ingrid. Look, this is a family do. I won't butt in.

Tom Yes, you will so butt in. Ellie, tell him.

Ellie You're very welcome, John.

Tom (*prompting her*) And he's to have a jar.

John I won't, thanks.

Ellie Oh.

It is a small, regretful "Oh", as if the matter were closed. Tom waits just long enough for her to insist. Again, here is a small point; it is almost as if the actors were unsure of a cue

Carlos Of course he will.

Tom That's telling him. (*Pouring, topping up*) Let us honour the day that's in it. Carlos, there's another bottle in the fridge.

Carlos crosses to the kitchen and exits

And open it in there. (*This with a look at Ingrid*)

Ingrid Oh, why?

John What about a toast?

Tom We've already had it. I said, "Here's to the house."

John Oh, Shakespearian!

Tom You're the brain, you're the intellectual, why don't you propose a toast?

John Certainly.

Tom So do it.

John You ready?

Tom This'll be good.

John Here's to the house . . .

Tom Ah, for the . . .

John (*silencing him*) May it never be quite big enough to hold the happiness that's inside it.

Tom He's a bloody genius.

Ellie Thank you, John.

Mary That's nice, that's witty, yes, it is. Ingrid, isn't that . . .

Ingrid has gone across to peer in through the kitchen door at Carlos opening the champagne

Honest to God, I think there's a bee in her.

Tom So what's new? Any word of the case?

Ellie Tom, John may not want to talk about it.

Tom What? Oh, sorry, love.

He stoops, lifts a carpet, real or imaginary, and, with foot or hand, sweeps an invisible substance under it. Ellie is angry

There . . . all gone. Okey-doke?

Ellie All I meant was . . .

Mary (*with affected innocence*) Case? Do you mean like in a summons?

There is a faint popping noise from the kitchen. Ingrid returns in triumph to her seat

Ingrid (*to Tom, a taunt*) Nyah.

John I'm taking an action against the St. Begnet's Board of Management. The school, that is.

Tom Wrongful dismissal.

John Well, suspension. (*Replying to Tom*) They say now it won't be heard till next year. Maybe even the year after.

Carlos comes in with the opened bottle

Tom You're kidding.

Carlos Dad, you're an innocent. You don't know the legal process. Will I pour this?

John "The law's delay, the insolence of . . ."

Tom So what happens in the meanwhile? I mean, what are you expected to live on?

John I can hustle a few grinds, mark exam papers, sweep the roads . . . no problem. And if I'm really stuck for a job, why else did the Irish invent England?

Ellie Yes, they say that over there they're crying out for . . .

Carlos No! Why should he? That's what 'ud suit Father Downey and the whole pack of them. Then they could say they ran him out of the town. No, you stand your ground. That's what you taught us.

John (*wryly; an echo of Part One*) Hoist with my own petard!

Tom I agree with Carlos.

Ellie clearly does not

Carlos He's too soft with them. (*To John*) If you don't hit back, they'll walk all over you. Do what they're afraid of . . . go to the media, create a stink.

John I am.

Carlos I mean, you have to put the boot in.

Ellie Now that'll do. It's John's concern, not yours.

Carlos I disagree.

Ellie I'm not arguing with you, I'm telling you.

Mary Your mammy is right. You'll only get yourself a bad . . .

John looks at Mary

(*A retreat*) I mean, you'd think people had nothing better to talk about.

John Yes, you would.

Mary (*embarrassed*) They'd give a body the sick.

Ingrid has been staring at John, fascinated

John (*his tone is friendly*) Hello, Ingrid.

She laughs, nervously

Are you well? Are you?

She looks, not at him, but at the others, vaguely, as if for help

Ingrid Not a feather out of me.

John I'm delighted. The reason I ask is, you have the look of a woman who was having her first sighting of a two-headed man.

Ellie John, don't be bold. No one is saying a word to you.

John Ingrid, we're all over the place . . . us men with two heads. Do you know what we're called? Do you know the name for us?

Ellie Now, Tom, talk to him.

John We're called "homo sapiens".

Ingrid (*softly, dismayed*) Oh, my God.

John (*comforting*) No, no. All it means is "modern man". Truly. "Man who thinks". Although we are divisible into two sub-species. It is the age, do you see, of specialization. So some of us are sapiens, and the ones left over are homos.

Ellie John!

John Or, as your good selves would probably call us, nancy boys.

Ellie (*on her feet*) Mammy and Ingrid, I'm sure you want to see the upstairs.

Mary The cheek of him.

Ellie (*urging her out*) Mammy!

Ingrid I never opened my mouth to him.

Mary Nor did I. It's the price of us for being broad-minded.

Mary, Ingrid and Ellie go out. As she goes Ellie gives John a look, not so much of anger as fond exasperation

John I'd better go.

Tom You'll do what he (*Carlos*) told you . . . you'll stand your ground. We'll have a scoop. (*To Carlos*) Are you a teetotaller?

Carlos Not today.

Tom (*pouring*) Terrible tack. I wish it was a pint.

John I wish it was pink gin.

Tom Do you know, if it cost fivepence, no one'd drink it. Good health.

They drink. Carlos splutters, rather like Ingrid

Jesus.

John I don't know what got into me. All I really need is for Ellie to show me the door.

Tom Ellie? Get off.

John That'd put the tin hat on it. Are you aware that you and she and Carlos and Madeleine . . . that as far as I'm concerned you lot are the Last Chance Saloon?

Carlos (*gasping*) Aunt . . . Aunt Ingrid is a pill.

Tom Mind your manners. I can say it; you can't.

John I saw that look on her face, and I went ape. It's the same look I see in the town. On my way here—ten minutes ago?—a couple of kids out of my own class at St. Begnet's . . . they quite openly called after me in the street: "Hey, Topsy!" Topsy. The boys didn't know when they christened me how right they were.

Tom John, you take too little too much to heart. In this day and age, who cares?

John (*out of despair*) It seems to me the whole damn world does.

Tom Not at all.

John What gets my goat is, I have no one to blame but me. I should have kept my mouth shut.

Tom You spoke out in a good cause.

John To hell with the cause. I got lonely.

Tom How?

John I mean, lonely for myself. For the half of me I kept locked away. God, was my timing ever off! The new enlightenment . . . I could taste it in the air . . . it was salt on the wind. So I carried that placard. I stood up to be counted. I was Houdini: one bound and I was out of the closet. Did you suspect I was gay?

Tom Never thought of it.

John (*to Carlos*) Did *you*? The other kids at school . . . did they know?

Carlos We wondered if you did.

John I was shown some of my fanmail, courtesy of Father Downey. "Did Pearse and Connolly die so that a pervert might contaminate our children?" Or: "Either the bum-boy leaves St. Begnet's or our Declan does." Jesus, I wouldn't mind, but I'm a fucking celibate. Sorry, Carlos.

Carlos (*stolidly*) It's your business.

John No, I mean . . . (*He lets it pass.*)

Tom If only . . . (*He pauses; his thoughts will not form*)

John Yes, if only. If only I'd waited another five or ten years . . . or won't the world have changed by then? Hang on . . . or if only this town was twice the size it is. Or if only I was a college lecturer instead of a corrupter of children.

Carlos You wait, John. You wait till we get dug into them.

John What was it you said? Create a stink?

Carlos Right on!

John Carlos . . . forget it.

Carlos Now come on . . .

John It's no use. People mean well, but they get tired . . . anger goes away. I'll be the darling of the liberals until they find a new toy and play with that for a while. No, that's unfair. There's a long line of old reliables . . . good causes, all waiting to be lost. (*With a crooked, shame-faced grin*) I was thinking of packing it in.

Tom How?

John (*almost mumbling*) Having . . . done with it.

Tom (*in alarm*) You what? You will, like hell . . . like hell you will.

Carlos What's he mean?

Tom (*staring at John*) Out of your bloody tree.

John It'd be one in the eye for them.

Carlos (*realizing*) Jesus.

Tom Will you quit it? Christ, I won't sleep tonight. No, listen to me . . . hang in there. Dying is . . .

Carlos (*shrilly*) Dying?

Tom . . . Dying is too easy.

John Is it? How is it?

Tom Because no one yet ever made a balls of it. (*With forced jollity*) Hey, that's not bad. Come on, have a jar. No more old guff. (*He picks up the bottle*) Carlos?

Carlos is staring at John, open-mouthed

Have you had enough?

Carlos (*still staring; he raises his empty glass for replenishing*) No.

In the garden area, the Assistant is looking off

Assistant Your one is coming . . . the young one.

Removals Man (*to us*) The story's not going right. It keeps twisting on me, same as a cat you'd try to put in a basket. When the head is in, a leg and a tail are out. Still, we're not starved for scenery . . . maybe we're going to the same place by a different road. And there's no new stories under the sun. The man that said that wasn't able to think up more than one.

Madeleine appears. She wears jeans, trainers and a sweatshirt with a wildlife motif

Good afternoon.

Madeleine Hi.

The Removals Man takes Madeleine by the arm to present her to us

Removals Man You would not think it to look at her, but at this moment she is a creature of the sea that has escaped from its hunters. Am I far wrong?

Madeleine (*smiling, a little shy*) Worse things I could be.

Removals Man She saves the whale and the dolphin, the hare and the fox and the battery hen.

Madeleine mutters

Excuse me?

Madeleine And otters.

Removals Man And otters. When she's at home, she is Madeleine. When she's out of it, her name is . . .

Madeleine Fax it, why don't you? Bloody Sister Veronique . . . she had to go rabbiting on about this old French book that's as long as a wet week and has madeleines in it. She said madeleine was a name for a . . . Can I go in now?

Removals Man Mais certainment.
Madeleine Bug off.

As in Part One, she finds that the Assistant is in her way

Excuse me.
Assistant How you doin'?
Madeleine (*snapping*) What?

Her response is so inauspicious that he would back off if he could, but he is aware that the Removals Man is watching

Assistant (*with feeble bravado*) Any chance?
Madeleine Of what? Oh, you mean any chance of *that*! No, I wouldn't say so. Sorry . . . I'm saving it for a human being.

She goes past him into the house, where she sees John, Tom and Carlos

Madeleine (*calling as she enters*) Anyone home?
John Look who's here . . . my dream girl.

Madeleine adopts an overdone, limp-wristed pose

Madeleine Hello, sailor!
John (*responding in kind*) Bitch.

They hug

Madeleine You all right, John? How are they treating you?
John Too seldom.
Madeleine God, he's like lightning. Hello, Dad. Hi, Carlos.
Carlos Hello, Bun.
Madeleine Don't call me that.
Tom What?
Madeleine Nothing. I want to have a quick gawk at my room.
Tom Your mother's showing the upstairs to your Granny and Aunt Ingrid.
Madeleine Oops. I'll hang on here, so. (*Seeing the champagne*) Can I have a sup of that?
Carlos I thought your lot were T.T.
Madeleine We have Saturdays off.

Tom is pouring out a glass

Dad, hurry up. She'll skin me. (*With mock-sentiment*) Ah, my first glass of champagne . . . what am I supposed to say?

John Genteel young ladies are required to giggle and say: "It tickles."

Madeleine Does it? (*Sipping*) Geroff, it does not. So how's the old poofter . . . are you well?

Tom (*outraged*) Madeleine . . . God in heaven.

John If He is, then I swear to Him I would kill for this child.

Tom No, but still . . .

John (*to Madeleine*) And, my darling, the next time you see the Reverend James Downey, P.P., you may tell him from me that the old poofter is fighting fit. It's a lie, but tell him.

Madeleine I *don't* see him. I don't go next or near the place.

Carlos Me, neither.

John (*looking at Tom*) Oh?

Tom It's their choice, they're old enough. (*To the children*) Just don't either of you go . . .

Madeleine Yeah, yeah . . . saying it out loud.

Tom *Bragging* about it . . . don't be so smart. Only a thick boasts about what he hasn't got.

John You tell 'em. (*moving*) Well . . . the middle-aged dog for the half-hard road.

Tom You're never off?

Madeleine Make him stay.

Tom You will. Bang of the latch.

John Ah, you're a . . .

Tom ⎫
John ⎭ (*together*) . . . terrible woman.

John suffers his glass to be refilled

John Did I, by the way, tell you, Madeleine . . .?

Madeleine Hello.

John . . . that you have become an out and out stunner?

Madeleine (*pleased*) Feck off.

John Much as you endeavour to hide it. Tom, you'll not have her for long.

Madeleine coughs consumptively

Tom Stop that. Mocking is catching.

John (*teasing her*) Any day now, a man with X-ray eyes will come along. He'll see through the jumble sale, and he'll say . . .

Madeleine Cheek of you. Leave me alone.

John Exactly.

Tom Hey, she's seventeen, give her a chance. Anyway, she's too busy saving the planet . . . aren't you, Mad?

Madeleine (*on this subject she is hyper-sensitive*) Am I?

Tom No, I don't fret about this one. Like we say in the shop, she has an indefinite shelf life.

Madeleine Oh, thank you bloody much.

Tom Now, now, I'm not . . .

Madeleine Yes, highly humorous. Well, I'm not saving the planet, Dad, no such thing. I'm just doing my bit to clean up the mess your lot made of it.

John (*amused; a touch uncomfortable*) Ow.

Madeleine (*to John*) Do you know, he sells battery eggs.

Tom responds wearily. We sense that it is an old bone of contention

Tom Tru-Valu does . . . I don't.

Madeleine Same difference. Poultry that's not free range, tenderized beef . . .

Tom Pardon me, miss, it bought up this house . . .

Madeleine (*not listening*) I mean, oh yuck.

Tom And it keeps *you*.

Madeleine (*dramatically*) Is that so? Then you've put blood on my hands.

Tom Have I? Good!

Father and daughter glare at each other at point-blank range

John (*meaning it*) That's nice. Lots of love. I like that.

Tom And in your passionate concern for animals, Madeleine, you might remember there are people in the world, too.

Madeleine Yes, worse luck.

John That's put me in my box.

Madeleine I don't mean you.

Carlos No, John is the exception. (*To John*) She has time for you on account of you're in the soup.

Madeleine No such thing.

Carlos Doesn't matter whether you talk, bark or go quack, you've got to be getting it in the neck before Bun'll stick up for you.

Madeleine That's a rotten lie.

Tom (*to Carlos*) Are you jarred?

Madeleine You're only a jealous boots because John likes me as well as you. And I don't answer to that name.

John What name?

Madeleine Never mind.

Carlos They call her Bun.

Madeleine (*with a sniff*) Because madeleine means a mouldy old sponge cake. Did *you* know that?

John I do, then. It's flavoured with rind of lemon, and it's a delicacy . . . like yourself. (*He puts his arms around her*) Come on . . . walk me to the door.

Tom You're not off?

John I have an instinct that the ladies won't come down till I pick up my handbag and depart. Ten to one they're on their knees by the front window.

Tom Will you stay and have a . . .

John No. Tom, square it with Ellie for me. Make it right.

Madeleine Why? What's up?

John I went and upset your Aunt Ingrid.

Madeleine (*with a malicious cackle*) Hih-hih-hih, you didn't.

John Truth is, since the trouble began, Ellie has been a bit . . . (*He makes an ambivalent gesture with one hand, palm downward*)

Tom How?

John A bit . . . polite.

Tom My wife . . . polite? See a doctor.

John Put in a word?

Tom (*an impatient nod, as if humouring him*) See you Monday in the new breakfast room. How about that?

John Trezz posh. 'Bye, Carlos.

Madeleine They call him Pedro.

Carlos, who has been on the verge of nodding off, comes to

Carlos What? . . . John, I'll pop round after tea.

John It'll be the waste of a fine evening. Still . . .

John and Madeleine move towards the front door. Carlos makes to pick up a champagne bottle

Tom So what's happening after . . . You put that down.

John 'Bye, my love . . . take care.

Madeleine John, it's true . . . I prefer animals to people any day, do you not?

John Couldn't agree more. Animals wait till they're hungry before they eat you.

John kisses Madeleine on the forehead. She returns indoors. John nods to the Removals Man and his Assistant; then he turns and looks at an upstairs window. He waves

John Woo-ee.

There are faint screams, off, from Mary and Ingrid

John goes gleefully on his way, almost skipping

In the living area, Tom picks up the two champagne bottles

Tom What's this about after tea?

Carlos (*sleepily*) I'm addressing envelopes.

Tom What for? Wake up.

Carlos Sorry? I talked John into writing to people who might weigh in on his side. You know . . . on the telly, all the bigwigs.

Tom Yes . . . well, your envelopes'll have to wait.

Carlos Who says?

Tom Son, we've been let down. The removals gang have picked today to go on a work-to-rule. Great, aren't they? It means that we either shift for ourselves or live in a mess till Monday.

Carlos Where's the harm in a mess? I don't mind.

Tom I do. I'm getting a few of the lads over from work . . . they'll take care of the heavy stuff.

Carlos Well, then!

Tom So I'm not having it put about the shop that Tom Noone's son and daughter were . . .

Madeleine Whoops . . . now hold on.

Tom . . . were too bloody high and mighty to stay home and do a hand's turn. (*Carelessly, he has missed her note of protest*) You'll pitch in, Maddie, I know that.

Carlos Dad, I'm helping John.

Tom Yes, out of bolshiness. You know it can wait.

Carlos Fine friend you are.

Tom Fine son you are.

Madeleine Dad, no offence, I really do mean that, but what world are you living in? I mean, you must be the only person alive who doesn't know that this evening is the Sellafield protest.

Tom The what?

Madeleine And sorry, but there's no way I'm missing it. Or would you prefer that the Irish Sea became a dumping ground for nuclear waste?

Tom Jesus, I give up.

Ellie has appeared. She will be followed in a moment by Mary and Ingrid

Ellie You give up what?
Tom Them. They love all humanity, people excepted.

From this point on, Tom is about to fight a losing battle on two fronts

Carlos That's telling us, Dad. Right on! (*He licks a finger and makes a score point in mid-air*)
Ellie (*quietly*) Mammy and Ingrid were afraid to come down. It was like being kept a prisoner.
Tom They weren't tied hand and foot . . . no need to lay it on John.
Carlos I'm going to take a look at my room.
Tom Not so fast. (*to Ellie*) This pair refuse to stay in this evening and help.
Ellie Then offer it up. They'll be less of a hindrance.
Mary John Turvey had no right to talk to Ingrid like that, no, he had not.
Ingrid And saying that word.
Tom What . . . "nancy-boy"?
Ellie Now don't you start.
Carlos Look, can I go upstairs.
Tom Yes, you can; no, you may not.
Carlos I bet John taught you that.

Tom gives him a two-finger salute and, almost in the same movement, turns on Ingrid

Tom Ingrid, the reason John said that word was because you were thinking it.
Ingrid Oh, I see. Now a body's thoughts aren't their own. (*With what for her is ferocity*) Well, it's what he is.

Carlos makes a slight involuntary move towards her; Tom puts out a hand, detaining him

Mary Ingrid, don't waste your passion. You and me are behind the times. The world we're living in, one half of them 'ud slaughter you in your bed, and the other half 'ud tell you: "Let on to enjoy it, you don't want to look narrow-minded." Well, they can be in the fashion all they like. What was unnatural yesterday is unnatural today, and if we chop and change, God doesn't. Say nothing, Ingrid.

Tom Right. Say nothing, Ingrid.

Carlos (*about to enter the fray*) I think . . .

Tom Yes, well, if you're that mad keen to see the upstairs, go.

Ellie First, why can't he and Madeleine stay in tonight? Not that they'll be missed, either of them, but I'd like to know what's so important?

Carlos opens and closes his mouth. Madeleine looks at him

Tom Cat's got his tongue. It's one of his pop concerts. (*To Carlos*) I said, go.

Carlos You coming Bun?

Madeleine scowls, then addresses the others

Madeleine The reason Carlos can't stay in is, he's going to . . .

Carlos All right . . . *Madeleine*, then.

Madeleine (*almost singing it*) . . . to the pop concert.

Madeleine and Carlos go out

Ellie senses a deception

Mary What for are you so soft? If you want them to do a thing, don't beg, *tell* them.

Ellie Mammy, you're the expert on how the world has changed. Do you not know? . . . you don't give orders any more. You ask politely. (*She loads the champagne bottles and assorted glasses back on the tray*)

Tom You look crossways at them and they move out and live in a squat.

Ellie It's true.

Mary What they need is a good slap.

Ellie Get sense.

Ellie carries the tray into the kitchen

Ingrid Mammy used to hit me, and I was none the worse for it.

Mary has drifted to the television set

Mary Is this plugged in? (*She switches it on*)

Tom Our two never gave us trouble. We were steeped.

From the television set a square of sharp light plays upon Mary's face. We either hear nothing at all or voices so faint as to be inaudible-probably it is the Oprah Winfrey Show

Mary It is. Yes, it is.

She switches the set off and turns away. Her attention has been caught, however, by what she has seen, and she switches it on again. The square of light once more appears: a small rectangular spotlight upon her face. She stands fascinated. She is not listening to Tom, who in any case is really speaking to himself. Ingrid, if she hears him, has her own interests to the fore

Tom They never either of them cost us a night's sleep. No drugs, no police at the door. Mind you, we had sense, we knew better than to ask for the moon and stars. Some parents expect kids to live in their pockets; then there's desolation when they won't. No, what I say is, whatever little they give you, be glad of it. And yet our two think the sun shines out of us. I'm not romancing. Mind, they don't kiss and hug, that's all out of style. Wet, they call it. Shyness, more like. No, we couldn't be closer.

A pause

Ingrid (*a pretence at lightness*) Hey, Tommy, tell me true. What did I ever do on you?

Ellie appears from the kitchen and stays at the entrance, looking on and listening

Tom Terrific kids. A credit to us.

Ingrid You never see me, but you put on a face, like I was a taste of what was gone bad. And we used to be great . . . we were so.

Tom makes no grimace of contradiction; he is hardly aware of her

I can remember you in short trousers. You went to the school on Kill Lane that's the Tandoori now. You called names after me in the town, and I cried. And Mammy went to Mr Mullen, the headmaster, and from then on when I passed you in the town, you said nothing, only crossed over, and then I cried even worse. Did Mr Mullen take the stick to you?

Tom nods, vaguely, his mind elsewhere

Then you met Ellie and me at that Exiles' Night Hop in Kilburn. I thought: him being here, out of all of London . . . ah no, not a coincidence, it must be what in the films they call destiny. And you asked me out and I went, except in the wind-up it was Ellie you took to live in Creebrishta. I mean, Tommy, I'm only saying. You've no call to be cross with me.

Tom (*not rudely, almost with pain*) You have so much foolishness.

Ellie comes into the room

Ellie Mammy, you're not watching that?
Ingrid I suppose she heard me. I don't care.
Mary Would you credit it? That woman there has dyed hair . . . ash blonde, she is. And the one beside her, with the snow-white hair, is the daughter.
Ellie What are they doing?
Mary They're Americans.
Ingrid Mammy, I want to go now.
Mary (*her eyes on the set*) Yes, love.
Ingrid If we walk quick, we can see it at home. Will you come on?

Mary is slow to tear her gaze away from the set

Mary All of a sudden there's another bee in her. Yes, we'll go. Have I my bag?
Ellie (*fetching it*) Yes. Now I don't want you saying you were hunted. You're welcome to stay.
Mary I know, I know. If I thought to the differ, we wouldn't budge. We'll have a proper evening when you're settled in and if we're asked.
Ingrid Mammy . . .
Mary Sure it's a nice house, yes, it is. (*To Ingrid*) Will you let me draw my breath? (*To Tom and Ellie*) God send yous good luck in it.
Ellie Tom, see Mammy and Ingrid out.
Ingrid 'Bye, Ellie. The champagne was only gorgeous.
Ellie Bye-bye, love. Mind yourselves, now.

Tom leads the way out a mite too readily

Tom Attagirls . . . here we go.
Mary God, I'm not a greyhound.

Tom shows them out of the house

Removals Man Ah, it's yourselves. Are the visiting hours over, then?

Mary (*snubbing him*) You're very pass-remarkable. Goodbye, so, Tom.

As Mary is setting off, Ingrid hangs back. She looks intimately at Tom

Ingrid, a minute ago you were panting to be off.

Ingrid (*softly*) 'Bye, Tommy.

She puts out her hand. He affects not to notice it, smiling at her with his teethe clenched. She is not put out; her smile as she turns to go lingers affectionately

Tom (*to himself*) Jesus.

Mary and Ingrid exit

As Tom makes to return indoors, the Removals Man has taken out his pocket watch

Removals Man Mr N., sir . . .

Tom Is that it? The home stretch, then?

Removals Man One more jump, sir, one more flick of the whip. They say the last ditch is always the worst.

Tom Yeah. I'll see you, then.

Removals Man Some day, please God.

They shake hands. Tom nods to the Assistant and goes into the house

Assistant The story's different, isn't it? You tried, but it didn't come out for you.

Removals Man Eamonn, it never does. With the Noones, only one thing is forever the same.

Assistant What's that, then?

The Removals man gives him a knowing grin and directs his attention to the interior of the house. He and the Assistant look on as Ellie, now wearing a pair of work gloves, unpacks an ornament. When she speaks about Ingrid, there is more curiosity in her voice and manner than annoyance

Ellie Tom, what the hell is going on with you and Ingrid?

Tom Between me and . . .?

Ellie Now don't start. I said *with* you and her, not *between* you. At least, give me that much sense. Well?

Tom Nothing.

Ellie Nothing. And yet you can't be in the same room with her.

Tom She . . .

Ellie She what?

Tom . . . gets on my wick.

Ellie How?

He does not answer

Tom, I've ignored it, I've let it pass. Now it's got so I'm afraid to have my own sister to the house. You and her, it's like the devil swimming in holy water. Was there a falling out, is that it?

Tom No.

Ellie Then why?

Tom We didn't fall out.

Ellie You like her, only you can't stand her, is that it?

He looks away impatiently

And I'm not taking Ingrid's part. God knows she can be a right pain. She's annoying and childish and silly, and there's times when I want to give her a good . . .

Tom (*suddenly*) Silly . . . yes. That's what it is . . . the silliness.

Ellie Is it, Tom? So what'll we do with her? I forget . . . do we still hang people for annoying us, or is that all done away with?

Tom Don't get shirty. You asked me, I'm telling you. (*Brooding*) Whatever house we live in, she walks into it, plonks herself down, opens her big mouth, and . . . (*He shakes the image from his mind*) In all this town there wasn't one girl, not one, who could hold a candle to her. Deny it to me . . . there was not. She was . . . (*reluctantly*) . . . she was the ideal. God, why else would we call names after her? I was working in Cussens's on Railway Road, and when it went to the wall, when Tru-Valu squeezed it out, I took the management course in London. And there she was again, you and her at that hop in Kilburn. You wouldn't believe how one person could light up a room. And now don't go putting words in my mouth . . . I never compared you and her.

Ellie How could you? I wasn't there.

Tom What? Yes, you . . .

Ellie Not for you, I wasn't.

Tom Oh. Anyway, all evening all she said was "yes" or "no" or "mmm". Getting a word out of her, you'd need pliers. It gave her a sort of air of mystery.

Ellie (*incredulously*) Ingrid?

Tom I asked her would she go out with me when the pair of us were back home. "Mmm". Five weeks of waiting. I saved up for it. I pushed the boat out. We had the first bottle of wine I ever bought. And after a glass of it, the shyness was gone, and there was the . . . (*He stops*)

Ellie The silliness.

Tom She opened that mouth of hers and the London Ingrid was gone. Killed, stone dead, and with her the one we used to call out after in the town. I don't forgive that in her, any more than I forgive me for taking the cover for the book. That night, after I left her home, I thought—I mean, not to harm a hair on her head—I thought, if only a romantic disease could have carried her off. But it didn't, and now she turns those eyes on me, like two cow flops in a field. And what I can't stand is, I know she's pitying me for having lost her. Have I upset you?

Ellie I'll get over it.

Carlos and Madeleine have come downstairs

(*Seeing them*) Hi, kids.

Carlos Mam . . . Dad, my room is fantastic . . . thank you.

Madeleine So is mine. Fabulous, it's really neat.

Ellie God, I wish it was.

Carlos Dad, we let you down.

Tom Oh?

Carlos Well, we came close. Now you tell your lads from work not to bother with our rooms. Whatever's to be done, we'll do it.

Madeleine Right. We're not parasites . . .

Carlos . . . We'll earn our keep.

Tom I wouldn't doubt either of you. I'm . . . delighted.

Carlos We'll make a start now and finish up this evening when Maddie comes home from town and I come . . . (*he blows it; finishing lamely*) . . . home from town. (*to Madeleine*) Right, Mad, will we have a go?

They go out. As they do so. Madeleine snorts with suppressed laughter and gives him a jab from behind for his blunder

Tom Ellie, you know what's the cruellest thing in the world? When your children are kind to you.

Ellie Tom . . . where is Carlos going this evening? Do you know?

Tom (*evasively, indicating the Removals Man*) The man says we have to finish up.

Ellie Because don't tell me he'll be at any pop concert.

Tom Look, I didn't want to say it in front of your mother and Ingrid, 'cause they'd have made a meal of it. He's only going over to John's digs.

Ellie (*tonelessly*) He's only going over to John's digs.

Tom To lend a hand. Himself and John have cooked up some kind of letter. Carlos's going to address the envelopes.

Ellie Tom . . .

Tom Ah-ha?

Ellie Is that it, then? Are you totally bereft of your senses?

Tom How?

Ellie You stand there and you calmly tell me you're letting your son go to that house?

Tom What house? Oh, now look . . . come on.

Ellie You're unbelievable. You are . . . you're . . .

Tom Well, if I am, it makes two of us. Do you think that for one solitary moment John Turvey would . . .

Ellie Don't be more stupid than you can help. I'm as fond of him as you are . . . or at least I was until he made a holy show of himself. Has it occurred to you what people will say? (*Pointing up, in a whisper*) About *him*.

Tom Town gossips, dirty minds, who cares?

Ellie I damn well care.

Tom Our friend—the man you happen to be running down—is the best in the world.

Ellie Is he? Then God help the rest of them.

Tom And you ought to be proud that your son is helping him.

Ellie Oh, I am, I am. Carlos'll be made for life. "Tom Noone's young lad . . . a walking legend, you know him well, of course you do. The poof."

Tom (*flaring up*) Shut up.

Ellie Or is it "the queer?"

Tom One day, Ellie . . . one day . . .

Ellie (*with venom*) One day, *what*? (*Simmering*) I mean, the cheek of him. Did he imagine that the town, all the kids' parents, that they'd thank him?

Tom No, he thought they might be broad-minded.

Ellie His mistake, then. (*Pause*) Do you mean that I'm not? Well, I beg to differ. I happen to think I am.

Tom Sure you are. Just as long as whatever it is stays on the far side of that door.

Ellie I never said I was a saint about it.

Tom is about to speak

Nor am I a devil, so don't make me out to be one. I don't care what John Turvey is or what he does or doesn't do. I'm not hard; I just want my peace and quiet. And my children are all I've got. The rest of it—the Mini, the holidays, the new house—they're the carrots that keep this donkey on the road. But no one, not you nor anyone like you, is taking from me the little I have left of those two. Now what you're going to do is this. You're going to tell my son to stay away from John Turvey.

Tom I can't do that.

Ellie Yes, you can, you bugger, and you will. Or I'll tell him for you.

Tom Go ahead. Remember what you said in this room: children don't take orders any more. So do it. Tell Carlos. Turn him against us.

She looks at him with hatred, thwarted and knowing that he is right

Ellie John Turvey will never set foot in this house again. At least I'll have my way in that.

Tom is shocked

Tom Hey . . . now come on. Have a heart.

Ellie You can meet him in the pub from now on . . . no one'll hinder you. Just don't bring him back here.

Tom What ails you?

Ellie Do you mind me? Because he won't be made welcome.

Tom You're someone else . . . this is not you. Carlos is to be kept away from John, and all for fear of what the Holy Joes of the town might say.

Ellie No.

Tom No? You just . . .

Ellie The Holy Joes can say what they like. It's not *talk* I'm afraid of.

Tom What, then? Afraid of John? Of who, then?

A moment's silence between them. Probably she would not put her fear into words

   Carlos appears

Carlos Bad news.

Ellie averts her face

   Maddie broke a looking-glass. So I hereby announce: total domestic misery until . . . (*a lightning piece of addition*) . . . nineteen-ninety-four. (*a stage-Chinese series of bows*) So velly solly!

   Carlos goes out again

Ellie turns and looks after him, even when he is not to be seen

Tom You won't believe what John said to us.
Ellie (*airily*) Not interested. Solly! (*She goes back to work at the tea-chests*)
Tom While you were upstairs, he . . .
Ellie Hey, I have work to do, my lad. So have you.
Tom He said that it was in his head . . .
Ellie It's moving day.
Tom . . . to do away with himself.

What he says seems to have no effect, except that for a few moments Ellie unwraps articles as if they were enemies to be destroyed

   Do you know what he called this place? The Last Chance Saloon. He said we were the only people he had left. You and me and Carlos and . . .
Ellie Oh, God.

It is a groan of anger, which Tom mistakes for another emotion

Tom I know, I know.
Ellie The bloody man . . . how dare he? He had no right, no right to say it to you, any more than you have the right to say it to me. Well, let him put a gun to his own head, if he wants, not to ours. (*Picking up an ornament*) Now this goes where? There!

She places it and dusts here hands briskly, as if a task had been disposed of. Tom's glance falls on the package brought by John

Tom Ellie. Ellie, what if he does it? What if he goes and . . .

Ellie I said, stop it. (*More calmly*) He won't. People who say they will never do, it's a well-known fallacy . . . well-known fact. Ask anyone.

She looks at the package which Tom is now holding

Tom "To Ellie and Tom." It's a prezzie from John.

Ellie (*affecting indifference*) Oh, yeah? (*Addressing an ornament*) So where's *your* new home to be? Tell us.

Tom (*opening the envelope*) "To Ellie and Tom . . . lest we forget." He even wrote your name first, see? Before mine. Oh, trust him. Will I see what it is?

Ellie ignores Tom

"Do, Tom." "Right so, Ellie." "We'll hurry, I can't wait." "I am, I am." He has no business buying us presents. The man has no job to go to. Still, we'll look at it and think of him.

The wrapping is off. It is a print of Munch's "The Scream." It is not what Tom had expected to see. Ellie, too, looks and stares at it

Yeah, it's very . . . what's the word. Forceful. Striking, wouldn't you say? Needs the right wall.

He looks at her, but she returns to her work, unyielding. He sets the picture down

No . . . no, better he should have waited, I'll give you that. Another three or four years, that's not so long. A small town, a small country . . . things can't be bullied and rushed. Give us time.

Ellie I'm going on forty. At my age, a person has the right to be left alone.

Tom is gravitating towards the television set. Ellie has won, he must now extricate himself with honour

Tom Because don't think we're not on the move. Good times are a-coming, you want to bet? I mean, sure . . . the kids are as good as gone from us. There's the odd whale needs saving, and the fella that's getting the short end of the stick and has to be stood up for, same as . . . (*he realizes that he is about to say "John"*) God, in our young day if we'd had the chances that pair have now, we'd have re-made the world. Did I tell you? . . . Maddie says she might go vegetarian.

The Removals Man has removed his apron and put his coat on

Removals Man Are you there, Eamonn? See what I mean? . . . the ending's no different.

The Assistant appears briefly

Assistant (*sceptically*) Oh, yeah?

Removals Man Son, it never will be. There's them that make history, and there's them that history makes. Like that decent woman said to him: we're the donkey, tomorrow's the carrot.

Tom is using the remote control to flick through the channels. The result is a babel of fragments of speech and music. The lights begin to dim so that we are left with only the flickering square of light from the TV on Tom's face.

Tom The important thing is to follow your star. As long as you go easy . . . don't get ahead of it.

From the confusion of sounds we hear a woman's voice: "Oh, Jerry, let's not ask for the moon, we have the stars!" Closing music—Max Steiner's—swells as we see Tom's face, his smile lost in the trouble-free world of the future

CURTAIN

FURNITURE AND PROPERTY LIST

Further dressing may be added at the director's discretion

PART ONE

On stage: Tea-chest 1. *In it:* books, draughtboard, Monopoly, portable radio
Tea-chest 2. *In it:* newspaper wrapped chinaware, bric-a-brac, ornaments
Fireside chairs
Table
Sideboard
Standard lamp
Dust-sheet
Empty packing case

Off stage: Sofa (**Removals Man** and **Assistant**)
Bed-linen (**Ellie**)
Brown paper bag. *In it:* six-pack of stout (**Tom**)
2 framed photographs (**Mary**)
Wrapped large framed print. *Attached to it:* envelope (**John**)
Tray with tea things and a plate of buttered brack (**Ellie**)
Patched-up tennis racket (**Madeleine**)

Personal: **Removals Man:** key ring with bottle opener
Mary: handbag. *In it:* handkerchief, broken pince-nez
John: fountain pen, 2 ball-point pens, gold fainne
Assistant: notebook
Tom: matches, money, two cigarette packs

PART TWO

On stage: Armchairs
Coffee table
2 tea-chests
Various household effects covered by a dust-sheet
Newspaper wrapped objects, including plants

Off stage: Good quality, deep sofa (**Removals Man** and **Assistant**)
TV set on purpose-made trolley (**Removals Man** and **Assistant**)
VCR (**Removals Man** and **Assistant**)
Music centre (**Removals Man** and **Assistant**)
2 expensive table lamps (**Removals Man** and **Assistant**)

Table (**Removals Man** and **Assistant**)
Silver-foil "Tru-Valu" supermarket bags (**Ellie**)
Six-pack of lager (**Assistant**)
Tray. *On it:* mixed drinking glasses (**Ellie**)
2 bottles of champagne (**Tom**)
Wrapped framed print. *Attached to it:* envelope with a card (**John**)
TV remote control (**Removals Man** and **Assistant**)

Personal: **Removals Man:** pocket watch, packet of cigarettes, matches, work gloves
Ingrid: handbag. *In it:* tissues
Assistant: notebook, work gloves

LIGHTING PLOT

Property fittings required: nil
2 interior settings

PART ONE

To open: Bring up general lighting; slowly fade out House lights

No cues

PART TWO

To open: Bring up general lighting, slowly fade out House lights

Cue 1   **Mary** switches on TV   (Page 71)
           Bring up a square of sharp light from theTV set on **Mary'**s *face*

Cue 2   **Tom** flicks through TV channels   (Page 80)
           Bring up a square of sharp light from the TV set on **Tom'**s *face, fade down general lighting*

EFFECTS PLOT

PART ONE

Cue 1	**Mary:** "The sea is the sea." *Dragging noise upstairs*	(Page 28)
Cue 2	**Ellie, Madeleine,** and **Karl** exit *Far-off thunderclap and the soft sound of rain*	(Page 40)

PART TWO

Cue 3	When the house is erected *Car door slams*	(Page 41)
Cue 4	**Mary:** "Do you mean like in a summons?" *Faint popping noise from the kitchen*	(Page 59)
Cue 5	**Mary** switches TV on, off, and on again *Sounds from TV as script page 71*	(Page 70)
Cue 6	**Tom** flicks through the channels *Sounds from TV as script page 80*	(Page 80)

PRINTED IN GREAT BRITAIN BY
THE LONGDUNN PRESS LTD., BRISTOL.